EYEWITNESS TRAVEL GUIDES

ARABIC
PHRASE BOOK

A Dorling Kindersley Book

LONDON, NEW YORK, MUNICH,
MELBOURNE, AND DELHI

Compiled by Lexus Ltd
Written by Mohammad Asfour

First published in Great Britain in 1998
by Dorling Kindersley Limited
80 Strand, London WC2R 0RL

Reprinted with corrections 2000, 2003
4 6 8 10 9 7 5

Dorling Kindersley books can be purchased in bulk quantities at
discounted prices for use in promotions or as premiums. We are
also able to offer special editions and personalized jackets, corporate
imprints, and excerpts from all of our books, tailored specifically to
meet your own needs. To find out more, please contact: Special Sales,
Dorling Kindersley Limited, 80 Strand, London WC2R 0RL;
Tel. 020 7010 3000.

A CIP catalogue record is available from the British Library.

ISBN 0 7513 2158 3

Printed and bound in China by Leo Paper Products Limited

see our complete catalogue at
www.dk.com

CONTENTS

PREFACE

This *Dorling Kindersley Eyewitness Travel Guides Phrase Book* has been compiled by experts to meet the general needs of tourists and business travellers. Arranged under headings such as Hotels, Driving and so forth, the Arabic words and phrases you may need to use are printed in familiar roman letters, following an easy to use imitated-pronunciation system that is fully explained on page 5.

Most sections in this book include boxes headed *Things You'll See*; these list the common words, signs, notices etc that you may see in Arabic script. The Arabic script is given alongside its Romanised pronunciation and the English translation.

Also included is a special section covering business talk. There is a 2,000-line mini-dictionary to help you form additional phrases, and the extensive menu guide translates over 300 Arab dishes. Guidance on aspects of the Arab way of life – points of etiquette, good manners and customs – will be found under the heading *Cross-Cultural Notes*.

Dorling Kindersley Eyewitness Travel Guides are recognised as the world's best travel guides. Each title features specially commissioned colour photographs, 3-D aerial views and detailed maps, cutaways of major buildings, plus information on sights, events, hotels, restaurants, shopping and entertainment.

Dorling Kindersley Eyewitness Travel Guides titles include:
Amsterdam · Australia · Sydney · Berlin · Budapest · California
Florida · Hawaii · New York · San Francisco & Northern California
Canada · France · Loire Valley · Paris · Provence · Great Britain
London · Ireland · Dublin · Scotland · Greece: Athens & the Mainland
The Greek Islands · Istanbul · Italy · Florence & Tuscany
Milan & the Lakes · Naples · Rome · Sardinia · Sicily
Venice & the Veneto · Jerusalem & the Holy Land · Mexico · Moscow
St Petersburg · Portugal · Lisbon · Prague · South Africa · Spain
Barcelona · Madrid · Seville & Andalusia · Thailand
Vienna · Warsaw

PRONUNCIATION

When reading the imitated pronunciation, stress the part of the word that is underlined. Pronounce each word as if it were an English word and you will be understood sufficiently well.

a, -ah	as in 'mad'
aa	as in 'far'
aw	as in 'law'
ay	as in 'day'
e	as in 'bed'
ee	as in 'sheen'
i	as in 'bit'
o	as in 'rob'
oo	as in 'food'
ŭ	as in 'book'

A	pronounced like a heavy, forced 'a', as in 'both of us – you And me!'
D	a heavily pronounced 'd'
gh	like a French 'r' – from the back of the throat
H	a heavily pronounced 'h'
kh	as in the Scottish pronunciation of 'loch'
q	a 'k' sound from the back of the mouth – as in 'caramel'
S, T	heavily pronounced 's, t'
th	as in 'thin'
Z	a heavily pronounced 'z'
'	this sounds like a small catch in the breath

When two vowels occur together each is pronounced separately. So for example in Ae- and aA each of the vowels are pronounced separately.

Note also that 'e' always has the same value – for example, in the Arabic be- the 'e' is pronounced as in the word 'bed'.

5

CROSS-CULTURAL NOTES

The Arab world comprises over twenty different states covering a vast geographical area. Manners and customs vary greatly depending upon each country's history, geography and climate, local conditions and the general level of development and national wealth. Nevertheless, there are several general cross-cultural differences which apply to all Arab countries to a greater or lesser degree and which should be borne in mind by all travellers to the Arab world whether they go there for business reasons or for pleasure.

Handshaking, and occasionally embracing, is the Arab greeting. If you are introduced to a group of Arabs you should shake them all by the hand in turn, starting with the most senior and ending with the youngest. When you address your Arab colleagues in business you should normally use their first name, ie Muhammad, Ali, Hussein etc, and prefix it by **ya sayed** ... (Mr ...). On the fewer occasions that you meet women in business you use **ya sayedah** instead. If the person you are addressing is particularly eminent or has some rank, you can substitute **ya ostaaz** ... (sir ...). You will normally be addressed by your first name prefixed in the same way, ie **ya sayed** John, and so on. In less formal contexts you will find people just use the first name prefixed by **ya** ...

Most socialising you do with Arabs will probably take place in the context of an hotel, restaurant or café. The rules of behaviour are just the same as they are in the West, although you will find that most Arabs have not acquired the habits of swearing, drinking and gaming that are so common elsewhere.

If you are invited into an Arab's home, however, you will find that in all probability traditional Arab customs and assumptions still hold sway. The most notable cultural difference is the partial or total segregation of women from all men but their husband and close family relations. As a male Western visitor to the more conservative countries you may not see many women during your visit – although this is changing in many large cities and in the more cosmopolitan countries such as Egypt. You will probably find that a meal has been timed to coincide with your visit. This will often come in the form of many dishes of food, and you will be encouraged to try all of them. Usually flat bread is served which can be used to scoop up the food. The meal may end with very small cups of bitter, strong black coffee or sweet tea served from a samovar. It is usual to take two or three cups and when you have had enough you just shake your cup before returning it to your host.

In large hotels you will certainly find Western-style toilets to sit on but in some other places you will only find the 'Turkish' variety. This is a porcelain base with foot supports and a hole. Although these are, debatably, not comfortable or easy to use there is no reason why they should be less hygienic than the Western variety. Try to carry a good supply of toilet paper or tissues with you at all times.

It is considered ill-mannered to use your left hand to shake hands or to eat with as it is thought of as the 'unclean' hand.

You will find that Arabs dress more smartly than many Westerners, especially young Arabs, and you should try and look smart too. It is best to avoid wearing shorts or anything particularly skimpy.

There is no getting away from the fact that women have a different status to men in Arab society, although this is gradually changing. Conditions for women vary greatly, although nowhere is it a good idea for a woman to travel alone. In the restaurants of Cairo it is quite acceptable for a woman to sip a beer. But in Saudi Arabia a woman may not even drive a car, let alone sit in a public place drinking anything.

For the alcohol-loving traveller the Arab world is definitely not the place. Alcohol is available in Egypt, Jordan and some other countries but it is absolutely forbidden in Saudi Arabia and some of the other states of the peninsula. Your trip to the Arab world is the ideal time to give your liver a holiday as well; fruit juices are cheap, plentiful and fresh.

USEFUL EVERYDAY PHRASES

Yes/no
naʌm/laa

Thank you
shokran

No, thank you
laa shokran

Please *(offering)*
tafaᴅal

Please *(asking for something)*
min faᴅlak

I don't understand
ma afham

Do you speak English/French/German?
hal tatakalam engleezee/faransee/almaanee?

I can't speak Arabic
ma aqdar atakalam ʌrabee

I don't know
ma aʌref

Please speak more slowly
law samaнt takalam sheway sheway

Please write it down for me
law samaнt, ektobha ʌla hazeh al-waraqah

My name is …
esmee …

How do you do, pleased to meet you
kayf Haalak, tasharafna be-meArefatak

Good morning
sabaaH al-khayr

Good afternoon
as-salaam Alaykum

Good evening
masa' al-khayr

Good night *(when going to bed)*
tesbaH Ala khayr

Good night *(leaving group early)*
maA as-salaamah *or* as-salaam Alaykum

Goodbye
maA as-salaamah

Excuse me, please
min faDlak, law samaHt

Sorry!
aasef!

I'm really sorry
aasef jeddan

Can you help me?
min faDlak, momken tosaAednee?

Can you tell me …?
min faDlak, momken taqool lee …?

Can I have …?
min faDlak, momken aakhoz …?

I would like …
oreed …

Is there … here?
fee … hona?

Where can I get …?
min wayn ajeeb …?

How much is it?
bekam?

What time is it?
as-saAh kam?

I must go now
laazem arooH fawran

I've lost my way
ana Dalayt aT-Tareeq

Cheers!
fee seHatak!

Do you take credit cards?
hal taqbal Visa, Access?

Where is the toilet?
wayn at-towaaleet/hamaam?

Go away!
emshee!

Excellent!
momtaaz!

**I've lost my passport/money/room key/traveller's cheques/
credit cards**
Dayyatu jawaaz safaree/fuloosee/meftaah ghurfatee/sheekaatee
assyaHeyya/beTaaqaatee

Where is the British embassy?
wayn is-sifaarit il-bireetaaneyya?

Is there wheelchair access?
hal fee madkhal li korsee bi-Ajalaat?

Are there facilities for the disabled?
hal fee tas-heelaat lil-Awajiz?

Are guide dogs allowed?
hal tasmaHoon bi-kilaab id-daleel?

THINGS YOU'LL HEAR

Afwan?/Afwan	Pardon?/You're welcome
al-Hamdo lellah, shokran – wa anta?	Very well thank you – and you?
be-ashoofak baAdayn	See you later
bejadd?	Is that so?
enshaallah	God (Allah) willing
kayf Haalak?	How are you?
kayf Haalak, tasharafna be-moqaabelatak	How do you do, nice to meet you
khalee baalak!	Look out!

→

maA as-salaamah	Goodbye
ma afham	I don't know
ma aAref	I don't understand
maalesh!	What does it matter!
saHeeH	That's right
shokran	Thanks
tafaDal	Here you are
tasharafna	You're welcome
ya moAlem!	Hey!

THINGS YOU'LL SEE

الدخول مجاناً	ad-dokhool majaanan	admission free
مغلق	moghlaq	closed
مغلق للعطلة	moghlaq lil-AoTlah	closed for holiday period
تفضل للداخل	tafaDDal lid-daakhil	come straight in
ماء للشرب	ma' lil-shorb	drinking water
مخرج الطوارئ	makhraj aT-Tawaaree'	emergency exit
مشغول	mashghool	engaged
شقة للإيجار	shaqqah lil-eejaar	flat for rent
ممنوع	mamnooA	forbidden
للبيع	lil-bayA	for sale
مصعد	mesAd	lift
رجال	rejaal	men

→

مسجد	masjed	mosque
ممنوع الدخول	mamnooA ad-dokhool	no admittance
المدينة القديمة	al-madeenah al-qadeemah	old city
مفتوح	maftooн	open
مواعيد العمل	mawaAeed al-Amal	opening times
خاص	khaas	private
اسحب	esнab	pull
ادفع	edfaA	push
محجوز	maнjooz	reserved
آثار / أطلال	aathaar/atlaal	ruins
أوكازيون	ookaazyoon	sale
مبيعات	mabeeAat	sales
سكوت / هدوء	sokoot/hodoo'	silence/quiet
تواليت / مرحاض	towaaleet/ merнaad	toilets
الخزينة	al-khazeenah	till
مواعيد الزيارة	mawaAeed az-zayaarah	visiting hours
دخول	dokhool	way in, entrance
خروج	khorooj	way out
احذر الدهان	eнzar ad-dehaan	wet paint
سيدات	sayedaat	women

DAYS, MONTHS, SEASONS

Sunday	yawm al-aHad
Monday	yawm al-ethnayn
Tuesday	yawm ath-tholatha'
Wednesday	yawm al-arbeAa'
Thursday	yawm al-khamees
Friday	yawm al-jomAh
Saturday	yawm as-sabt

January	yanaayer
February	febraayer
March	maars
April	ebreel
May	maayo
June	yoonyo
July	yoolyo
August	aghosтos
September	sebtember
October	oktoober
November	noofember
December	deesember

Spring	al-ar-rabeeA
Summer	as-sayf
Autumn	al-khareef
Winter	ash-sheta'

Christmas	al-kreesmaas/Aeed al-meelaad
Christmas Eve	laylat al-kreesmass
New Year	ra'es as-sanah
New Year's Eve	laylat ra'es as-sanah
Aeed alfeтr	feast at the end of Ramadan
awwal moHarram	Muslim New Year's Day
mawlood al nabee	Mohammad's birthday
ramaDaan	Ramadan (Muslim month of fasting)

NUMBERS, THE CALENDAR

0	.	sefr		
1	١	waaHed		
2	٢	ethnayn		
3	٣	thalaathah		
4	٤	arbaAh		
5	٥	khamsah		
6	٦	settah		
7	٧	sabAh		
8	٨	thamaaneeyah		
9	٩	tesAh		
10	١.	Asharah		
11	١١	Hedaash		
12	١٢	etnaash		
13	١٣	thalaathaash		
14	١٤	arbaAtaash		
15	١٥	khamastaash		
16	١٦	settaash		
17	١٧	sabaAtaash		
18	١٨	thamaantaash		
19	١٩	tesAtaash		
20	٢.	Aeshreen		
21	٢١	waaHed wa Aeshreen		

22	٢٢	ethnayn wa Aeshreen	
30	٣.	thalaatheen	
31	٣١	waaHed wa thalaatheen	
32	٣٢	ethnayn wa thalaatheen	
40	٤.	arbaAeen	
50	٥.	khamseen	
60	٦.	setteen	
70	٧.	sabAeen	
80	٨.	thamaaneen	
90	٩.	tesAeen	
100	١..	me'ah	
110	١١.	me'ah wa Asharah	
200	٢..	me'tayn	
300	٣..	thalaathme'ah	
400	٤..	arbaAme'ah	
500	٥..	khamsme'ah	
600	٦..	setme'ah	
700	٧..	sabAme'ah	
800	٨..	thamaanme'ah	
900	٩..	tesAme'ah	
1,000	١...	alf	
2,000	٢...	alfayn	

10,000	Asharat aalaaf
1,000,000	malyoon

You will notice that, while Arabic words are written from right to left, Arabic numerals are written from left to right. You will also notice that no commas are inserted to show thousands. A comma is used as a decimal point instead.

The Calendar

		16th	as-saades Ashar
1st	al-awal	17th	as-saabeA Ashar
2nd	ath-thaanee	18th	ath-thaamen Ashar
3rd	ath-thaaleth	19th	at-taaseA Ashar
4th	ar-raabeA	20th	al-Aeshroon
5th	al-khaames	21st	al-Haadee wa al-Aeshroon
6th	as-saades	22nd	ath-thaanee wa al-Aeshroon
7th	as-saabeA	23rd	ath-thaaleth wa al-Aeshroon
8th	ath-thaamen	24th	ar-raabeA wa al-Aeshroon
9th	at-taaseA	25th	al-khaames wa al-Aeshroon
10th	al-Aasher	26th	as-saades wa al-Aeshroon
11th	al-Haadee Ashar	27th	as-saabeA wa al-Aeshroon
12th	ath-thaanee Ashar	28th	ath-thaamen wa al-Aeshroon
13th	ath-thaaleth ashar	29th	at-taaseA wa al-Aeshroon
14th	ar-raabeA Ashar	30th	ath-thalaathoon
15th	al-khaames Ashar	31st	al-Haadee wa ath-thalaathoon

TIME

today	al-yawm
yesterday	ams
tomorrow	bokrah
the day before yesterday	awal ams
the day after tomorrow	baAd bokrah
this week	haza al-osbooA
last week	al-osbooA al maaDee
next week	al-osbooA al-qaadem
this morning	haza as-sabaaH
this afternoon	al-yawm baAd az-zohr
this evening	haza al-masa'
tonight	al-laylah
yesterday afternoon	ams baAd az-zohr
last night	laylat ams
tomorrow morning	bokrah fees-sabaaH
tomorrow night	bokrah feel-masa'
in three days	fee khelaal thalaathat ayaam
three days ago	monzo thalaathat ayaam
late	mota'akhar
early	badree
soon	qareeban
later on	baAdayn
at the moment	al-Heen
second	thaaneeyah
minute	daqeeqah
one minute	daqeeqah waaHedah
two minutes	daqeeqatayn
quarter of an hour	robA saAh
half an hour	nosf saAh
three quarters of an hour	saAh ela robA
hour	saAh
that day	daak al-yawm
every day	kol yawm
all day	Towaal al-yawm
the next day	al-yawm at-taalee

TELLING THE TIME

To say 'the time is X o'clock' you simply use the words **as-saAh** followed by the number of the hour. For example, 'it is nine o'clock' is **as-saAh tesAh** and 'it is five o'clock' is **as-saAh khamsah**.

To say it is quarter past the hour you add the words **wa robA** (and a quarter) to the hour. To say it is twenty past the hour you add the words **wa thulth** (and a third) to the hour. To say it is half past you add the words **wa nesf** (and a half) to the hour just passed.

Times between half past and the following hour use the following hour as a base. **Wa** becomes **ela** (minus). 'It is twenty to three' is **as-saAh thalaathah ela thulth** (it is three o'clock minus a third). Similarly a quarter to the hour is expressed by the word for that hour with the words **ela robA** (minus a quarter).

To give the time to the minute you either add **wa X daqaa'eq** for times up to the half hour, or use the following hour and **ela X daqaa'eq** if the time is between the half hour and the following hour.

The twenty-four hour clock is mainly used for timetables rather than general conversation. To make it clear that a time is in the morning you can add **sabaaHan**. For the afternoon you can use **baAd az-zohr**. Times in the evening may be made unambiguous by adding **masa'an**.

am	sabaaHan
pm	baAd az-zohr
one o'clock	as-saAh al-waaHedah
ten past one	waaHedah wa Asharah
quarter past one	waaHedah wa robA
half past one	waaHedah wa nosf
twenty to two	ethnayn ela thulth
quarter to two	ethnayn ela robA
two o'clock	as-saAh ethnayn

13.00 (1 pm)	as-saAh waaHedah baAd az-zohr
16.30 (4.30 pm)	as-saAh arbaAh wa nosf
at half past five	as-saAh khamsah wa nosf
at seven o'clock	as-saAh sabAh
noon	as-saAh ethnaash zohran
midnight	as-saAh ethnaash masa'an

HOTELS

The business traveller in the Arab world will have no difficulty in finding suitable accommodation in any Arab country. All major cities have high-quality hotels – at least three-star equivalent – but it is advisable to make a reservation beforehand. These quality hotels levy a service charge of between 10% and 15% which is added to the bill, and bell hops and waiters should be tipped separately. It is worth knowing that there is a particularly hefty mark-up on outgoing telephone and fax calls, particularly international ones, and you might wish to avoid this burden by being called instead. Some of the smaller states such as Qatar, Kuwait and Oman have only this type of quality hotel. Foreign visitors are almost exclusively business travellers and hence there has been no demand for more modest accommodation facilities.

In those countries – such as Egypt, Syria, Jordan, Morocco and Tunisia – which have a well developed tourist industry there is a much wider choice of accommodation to suit all pockets. Hotels range from the luxurious to the very basic. It is fair to say that if a hotel can be pre-booked from abroad then it is likely to meet minimum standards of hygiene and comfort.

The traveller who is back-packing or on a modest budget will find no shortage of cheap hotel accommodation in these countries. Hotels are usually grouped together in one part of town and it is always best to spend as much as possible on accommodation to ensure that your stay is as pleasant as you can afford.

While English is always spoken in the very large hotels, you will find that you really need a phrase book in medium and small establishments, particularly away from larger towns and cities. Bon voyage and good luck!

Useful Words and Phrases

bathroom	Hamaam
bed	sareer
bedroom	ghorfat nawm
breakfast	foToor
dining room	ghorfat as-sofrah
dinner	Ashaa'
double room	ghorfah mozdawajah
foyer	saalah
hotel	fondoq
key	meftaaH
lift	mesAd
lounge	saalah
lunch	ghadaa'
manager	modeer
receptionist	mowazzaf al-esteqbaal
restaurant	maTAm
room service	khedmat al-ghoraf
single room	ghorfah be-sareer waaHed
twin room	ghorfah be-sareerayn

Have you any vacancies?
fee Andak ghoraf khaaleeyah?

I have a reservation
Andee Hajz

I'd like a single room
oreed ghorfah be-sareer waaHed

I'd like a double room
oreed ghorfah mozdawajah

I'd like a twin room
oreed ghorfah be-sareerayn

I'd like a room with a bathroom
oreed ghorfah be-Hammam

I'd like a room with a balcony
oreed ghorfah be-balakoonah

Is there satellite/cable TV in the rooms?
hal fee telivizyoon saatelayt/kaabil fil-ghorfah?

I'd like a room for one night
oreed ghorfah le-modat laylah waaHedah

I'd like a room for three nights
oreed ghorfah le-modat thalaath layaalee

What is the charge per night?
kam seAr al-ghorfah le-modat laylah waaHedah?

Is there a reduction for children?
hal fee takhfeedh lil-aTfaal?

Can I see the room?
momken ashoof al-ghorfah?

Is there a highchair/cot/baby changing room?
hal fee korsee Alee/sareer/ghorfah li-taghyeer at-Tifl?

I don't know yet how long I'll stay
ma aAref beD-Dabt modat al-eqaamah

When is breakfast?
mata meAad al-foToor?

When is dinner?
mata meAad al-Ashaa'?

Would you have my luggage brought up?
momken torsel shonaTee fawq?

Please call me at … o'clock
law samaHt tasel bee as-saAh …

Can I have my breakfast in my room?
momken tajeeb lee al-foToor fee ghorfatee?

Can you warm this bottle/baby food for me?
momken tasakhkhanli az-zujaajah/TaAm ar-raDeeA?

I'll be back at … o'clock
sa-arjaA as-saAh …

My room number is …,
ghorfatee raqm …

I'm leaving tomorrow
ana maashee bokrah

Can I have the bill, please?
momken al-faatoorah law samaHt?

I'll pay by credit card
sa-adfaA al-faatoorah Visa, Access

I'll pay cash
sa-adfaA naqdan

Can you get me a taxi?
momken tajeeb lee taaksee?

Can you recommend another hotel?
momken towsee be-fondoq aakhar?

There's no water
ma fee miy<u>aa</u>h

There's no toilet paper
ma fee w<u>a</u>raq towaal<u>ee</u>t

THINGS YOU'LL SEE		
حمّام	Ham<u>aa</u>m	bath
مبيت وفطور	mab<u>ee</u>t wa foToor	bed and breakfast
فاتورة	faat<u>oo</u>rah/hes<u>aa</u>b	bill
فطور	foT<u>oo</u>r	breakfast
مخرج الطوارئ	khor<u>oo</u>j aT-Taw<u>aa</u>re'	emergency exit
إقامة كاملة	eq<u>aa</u>mah k<u>aa</u>melah	full board
الطابق الأرضي	aT-T<u>aa</u>beq al-<u>a</u>rDee	ground floor
نصف إقامة	nesf eq<u>aa</u>mah	half board
مصعد	mesAd	lift
غداء	ghad<u>aa</u>'	lunch
كل الغرف محجوزة	kol al-ghoraf maHj<u>oo</u>zah	no vacancies
رقم	raqam	number
اسحب	<u>e</u>sHab	pull
ادفع	<u>e</u>dfaA	push
استقبال	esteqb<u>aa</u>l	reception
حجز	Hajz	reservation ⟶

مطعم	**maTAam**	restaurant
غرفة	**ghorfah**	room
دوش	**dosh**	shower
تواليت / مرحاض	**towaaleet/ merHaaD**	toilet

THINGS YOU'LL HEAR

ana mota'ssef, kol al-ghoraf maHjoozah
I'm sorry, we're full

ma fee ghoraf be-sareer waaHed baaqeeyah
There are no single rooms left

ma fee ghoraf be-sareerayn baaqeeyah
There are no double rooms left

le-modat kam laylah?
How many nights?

esmak ay/shoo esmak?
What is your name?

kayf be-tadfaʌ al-fatoorah?
How will you be paying?

law samaHt edfaʌ moqadaman
Please pay in advance

momken ashoof jawaazak law samaHt?
Can I see your passport, please?

DRIVING

Generally, visitors to the Arab world will not be driving themselves around. If you do hire a car, try to make sure you know the route and, if travelling across desert roads, are equipped with additional petrol and provisions. The rule of the road everywhere is to drive on the right. Some countries accept a British driving licence for a short period (1–2 months), others require an international driving licence while a few insist on a driver obtaining a temporary national licence locally. In Saudi Arabia women are not permitted to drive on their own except within foreign compounds and it is not recommended anywhere at all. Full and up-to-date details of local requirements can always be obtained from an embassy or consulate of the relevant Arab country abroad, or from a national motoring organisation (such as the AA or the RAC in Britain). Although third party insurance is not always compulsory a prudent driver will never drive without cover – inability to pay damages has resulted in a prison sentence in many cases in the past.

Motorways and expressways linking major cities are kept in a fairly good state of repair but once you drive off these main routes you will find that road-repairing and general road maintenance is patchy and frequently non-existent. Traffic control tends to be carried out in cities by traffic policemen as well as traffic lights – or often a combination of both. You can be fined on the spot for traffic offences – chiefly speeding.

You will find that motorists use their horns a great deal in traffic jams and at intersections and you will need to acquire this habit to hold your own on the roads.

SOME COMMON ROAD SIGNS

شارع غير مرصوف	shaareA ghayr marsoof	bad surface
احترس من القطارات	eHtares men al-qeTaaraat	beware of the trains
موقف سيارات	mawqef sayaaraat	car park
عبور غنم وأبقار	Aoboor ghanam wa abqaar	cattle crossing
احترس	eHtares	caution
تقاطع طرق	taqaaTOA Toroq	crossroads
جمرك	jomrok	customs
خطر	khaTar	danger
منحنى خطر	monHana khaTar	dangerous bend
ملتقى طرق خطر	moltaqa Toroq khaTar	dangerous junction
تحويلة	taHweelah	diversion
نهاية طريق السفر	nehaayat Tareeq as-safar	end of motorway
إسعافات أولية	esAafaat awaleeyah	first-aid
للسيارات الثقيلة	lel-sayaaraat ath-thaqeelah	for heavy vehicles
جراج	garaaj	garage
افسح الطريق	efsaH aT-Tareeq	give way
اطفئ المصابيح الأمامية	eTfee al-masaabeeH al-amaameeyah	headlights off

→

اشعل المصابيح الأمامية	ashAel al-masaabeeh al-ammaameeyah	headlights on
معبر قطارات	maAbar qiTaaraat	level crossing
انعطاف عربات النقل	enAeTaaf Arabaat an-naql	lorries turning
طريق سفر (تدفع فيه الرسوم)	Tareeq safar (todfaA feehee ar-rosoom)	motorway (with toll)
ممنوع الدخول	mamnooA ad-dokhool	no entry
ممنوع التخطي	mamnooA at-takhaTe	no overtaking
ممنوع الوقوف	mamnooA al-woqoof	no parking
ممنوع التجاوز	mamnooA at-tajaawoz	no trespassing
شارع اتجاه واحد	shaareA ettejaah waaHed	one-way street
موقف السيارات	mostawdaA as-sayaaraat	parking
مشاه	moshaah	pedestrians
بنزين	banzeen	petrol
محطة بنزين	moHaTat banzeen	petrol station
منطقة وقوف محددة	menTaqat woqoof moHadadah	restricted parking zone

→

أشغال طرق	**ashgh<u>aa</u>l Toroq**	roadworks
مدرسة	**madr<u>a</u>sah**	school
محطة خدمة	**moH<u>a</u>Tat kh<u>e</u>dmah**	service station
هدئ السرعة	**had<u>ee</u>' as-s<u>o</u>rAh**	slow
قف!	**qeff!**	stop!
نفق	**n<u>a</u>faq**	subway, tunnel
رسوم	**ros<u>oo</u>m**	toll
وسط المدينة	**w<u>a</u>saT al-mad<u>ee</u>nah**	town centre
شارع غير مستوٍ	**sh<u>aa</u>reA ghayr most<u>a</u>wee**	uneven surface

USEFUL WORDS AND PHRASES

automatic	awtoom<u>aa</u>teek
boot	sh<u>a</u>nTat as-say<u>aa</u>rah
breakdown	A<u>o</u>Tol
brake	far<u>aa</u>mel
car	say<u>aa</u>rah/arabiyah
caravan	kaarav<u>aa</u>n
clutch	debreey<u>aa</u>j
crossroads	taq<u>aa</u>ToA
to drive	yas<u>oo</u>q
engine	moH<u>a</u>rrek
exhaust	shakm<u>aa</u>n
fanbelt	sayr al-marw<u>a</u>Hah
garage *(for repairs)*	gar<u>aa</u>j meekaan<u>ee</u>kee
(for petrol)	maH<u>a</u>TTat banz<u>ee</u>n
gear(s)	geer
junction *(motorway)*	taq<u>aa</u>ToA
licence	r<u>o</u>ksah

lights (*head*)	anwaar amaameeyah
(*rear*)	anwaar khalfeeyah
lorry	looree
manual	Aadee
mirror	meraayah
motorbike	mootooseekl
motorway	Tareeq safar
number plate	lawHat arqaam
petrol	banzeen
road	Tareeq
to skid	yazleq
spares	qeTAA ghiyaar
speed	sorAh
speed limit	Had as-sorAh
speedometer	Adaad as-sorAh
steering wheel	derekseeyoon
to tow	yasHab
traffic lights	eshaaraat moroor
trailer	maqToorah
tyre	taayer
van	sayaarah vaan
wheel	Ajalah
windscreen	zojaaj
windscreen wipers	masaaHaat zojaaj as-sayaarah

I'd like some petrol/oil/water
oreed banzeen/zayt/miyaah

Fill her up, please!
fawelha law samaHt!

I'd like 10 litres of petrol
oreed Asharah leeter banzeen

Would you check the tyres, please?
momken toshayek at-tawaayer law samaHt?

Where can I park?
wayn owaqqef as-sayaarah?

Can I park here?
momken owaqqef as-sayaarah hona?

Is this the road to …?
hal haza howa aт-тareek le …?

Where is the nearest garage?
wayn aqrab garaaj?

DIRECTIONS YOU MAY BE GIVEN

seedah	straight on
Ala al-yasaar	on the left
leff yasaar	turn left
Ala al-yameen	on the right
leff yameen	turn right
awal shaareA Ala al yameen	first on the right
thaanee shaareeA Ala al-yasaar	second on the left
baʌd al …	past the …

Do you do repairs?
hal tosaleHoon sayaaraat?

Can you repair the clutch?
hal taqdar tosalleH ad-debreeyaaj?

How long will it take?
qad aysh waqt be-taakhoz?

There is something wrong with the engine
fee khalal feel-moHarrek

The engine is overheating
al-moHarrek be-taskhan ziyaadah An al-lozoom

The brakes are binding
al-faraamel qaabeDah

I need a new tyre
oreed taayer jadeed

I'd like to hire a car
oreed asta'jer sayaarah

Is there a mileage charge?
hal honaak ajer le kol meel?

Can we hire a baby/child seat?
momkin nasta'jir korsee lir-RaDeeA/lit-Tifl?

THINGS YOU'LL HEAR

hal tor<u>ee</u>d say<u>aa</u>rah awtoom<u>a</u>at<u>ee</u>k w<u>a</u>la ʌad<u>ee</u>yah?
Would you like an automatic or a manual?

m<u>o</u>mken ash<u>oo</u>f rokhs<u>a</u>tak?
May I see your licence?

THINGS YOU'LL SEE

الطريق البطيء	aт-тar<u>ee</u>q al-baт<u>ee</u>'	crawler lane
ديزل	d<u>ee</u>zel	diesel
تحويلة	taнw<u>ee</u>lah	diversion
خروج	khor<u>oo</u>j	exit
بنزين سوبر	banz<u>ee</u>n s<u>oo</u>per	four star
طريق سفر	тar<u>ee</u>q s<u>a</u>far	motorway
مفترق طريق السفر	moft<u>a</u>req тar<u>ee</u>q as-s<u>a</u>far	motorway junction
زيت	zayt	oil
مستوى الزيت	most<u>a</u>wa az-zayt	oil level
طابور	т<u>aa</u>b<u>oo</u>r	queue
تصليح	tasl<u>ee</u>н	repair
بنزين متوسط	banz<u>ee</u>n mutaw<u>a</u>siт	three star
أزمة مرور	<u>a</u>zmat mor<u>oo</u>r	traffic jam
بنزين عادة	banz<u>ee</u>n ʌ<u>aa</u>da	two star
هواء الإطارات	haw<u>aa</u>' al-iт<u>aa</u>r<u>aa</u>t	tyre pressure

RAIL TRAVEL

The quality, or even existence, of rail travel varies greatly in the Arab world. With the exception of Saudi Arabia there are no railways at all in the states of the peninsula: the Yemen, Oman, the United Arab Emirates, Qatar, Bahrain and Kuwait. In Saudi Arabia there is one express railway line linking the capital Riyadh and the Arabian Gulf port of Damman. This train carries air-conditioned coaches and provides a comfortable ride into the oil-producing region of the country.

In Jordan, Syria, Lebanon and Iraq there are passenger rail services but these are slow, irregular and rarely air-conditioned. They are much used by local people and are very cheap. If you want to travel a little faster you could use the bus and coach services available in those countries. And there are also shared taxi services which ply between the larger towns and cities.

The same situation is true of almost all North African Arab states: Morocco, Algeria, Tunisia and Libya.

When it comes to travel by rail in the Arab world, Egypt is better than most countries. It has two main routes: a line running from the Mediterranean port of Alexandria to the capital Cairo; and a line running from Cairo through the ancient city of Luxor near the Valley of the Kings right up to the southern town of Aswan at the foot of the Aswan dam. First-class travel, which is cheap compared with Western services, is recommended since it is completely air-conditioned and equals European services in most respects. Many travellers on this line use the excellent sleeper trains which travel overnight and save you spending a day on the train. The first-class cabins are very comfortable. Whichever class you decide to travel you will find the trains punctual and the trip affords spectacular views of the Nile scenery and landscape. Travellers to Egypt who have any time to spare really should make an effort to travel on at least part of the Nile-side railway.

In Saudi Arabia women should not travel unaccompanied by a man and elsewhere women are not advised to travel alone by rail. The reason is not that women may be bothered by men, but that Arab custom does not like to see women out on their own. You will find separate ticket counters for men and women in many railway stations.

USEFUL WORDS AND PHRASES

air conditioning	takyeef al-hawaa'
booking office	maktab Hajz at-tazaaker
buffet	boofay
carriage	Arabah
compartment	maqsoorah
connection	tawseelah
dining car	Arabat al-ghazaa'
emergency brake	selselah le-tawqeef al-qeTaar
engine	qaaTerah
entrance	madkhal
exit	makhraj
first class	darajah oolah
to get in	yasAd
to get out	yanzel
guard	Haares
indicator board	lawHat al-bayaanaat
left luggage	maktab al-Haqaa'eb al-matrookah
lost property	al-mafqoodaat
luggage rack	raff waDA al-Haqaa'eb
luggage trolley	Arabah sagheerah le-naql al-Haqaa'eb
luggage van	Arabat naql al-Haqaa'eb
platform	raseef
pullman	looks
railway	sekkah Hadeedeeyah
reserved seat	maqAd maHjooz
restaurant car	Arabat al-maTam
return ticket	tazkarat zehaab wa Awdah
seat	maqAd
second class	darajah thaaneeyah

single ticket	tazkarat zehaab faqaт
sleeping car	Arabat nawm
station	maнaттah
station master	naazer al-maнaттah
ticket	tazkarah
ticket collector	moнassel at-tazaaker
timetable	jadwal mawaAeed
tracks	qoдbaan
train	qeтaar
waiting room	ghorfat al-entezaar
window	shobaak

When does the train for ... leave?
emta yaqoom al-qeтaar ellee raayeн le ...?

When does the train from ... arrive?
emta yasel al-qeтaar ellee jaay men ...?

When is the next train to ...?
emta al-qeтaar at-taalee le ...?

When is the first/last train to ...?
emta awal/aakher qeтaar le ...?

What is the fare to ...?
be-kam at-tazkarah le ...?

Do I have to change?
hal laazem oghayyer al-qeтaar?

Does the train stop at ...?
hal al-qeтaar yaqef fee maнaттat ...?

How long does it take to get to ...?
aysh тool al-masaafah le ...?

A single ticket to … please
law samaHt, tazkarat zehaab le …

A return ticket to … please
law samaHt, tazkarat zehaab wa Awdah le …

Do I have to pay a supplement?
hal laazem adfaA mablagh eDaafee?

I'd like to reserve a seat
oreed aHjez maqAd law samaHt

Is this the right train for …?
hal haza howa al-qeTaar le …?

Is this the right platform for the … train?
hal haza howa ar-raseef lel-qeTaar …?

Which platform for the … train?
wayn ar-raseef lel-qeTaar ellee raayeH …?

Is the train late?
hal al-qeTaar less mota'akhar?

Could you help me with my luggage, please?
momken tosaAednee fee shayl shonaTee law samaHt?

Is this a non-smoking compartment?
hal hazehe maqsoorah mamnooA feeha at-tadkheen?

Is this seat free?
hal haza al-maqAd khaalee?

This seat is taken
haza al-maqAd mashghool

I have reserved this seat
ana Hajazet haza al-maqAd

May I open/close the window?
momken aftaH/aqfel ash-shobaak?

When do we arrive in ...?
emta nasel ...?

What station is this?
hazehe ay maHaTTah?

Do we stop at ...?
hal al-qeTaar yaqef fee maHaTTat ...?

Is there a restaurant car on this train?
hal fee Arabat maTAm fee haza al-qeTaar?

THINGS YOU'LL SEE

وصول	wos**oo**l	arrivals
عربة	Arabah	carriage
المحطة المركزية	al-moHaTTah al-markaz**ee**yah	central station
تغيير عملة	taghy**ee**r Aomlah	currency exchange
تأخير	ta'akh**ee**r	delay
رحيل	raH**ee**l	departures
لا يقف في...	laa yaqef fee ...	does not stop in ...
لا تطل برأسك خارج الشباك	laa taTol be-ra'esak khaarej ash-shob**aa**k	do not lean out of the window

→

فرملة طوارئ	**farmalah Tawaari'**	emergency brake
مشغول	**mashghool**	engaged
مدخل	**madkhal**	entrance
مخرج	**makhraj**	exit
معلومات	**maAloomaat**	information
رحلة	**reHlah**	journey
حقائب متروكة	**Haqaa'eb matrookah**	left luggage
قطار محلي	**qeTaar maHalee**	local train
كشك الجرائد	**koshk al-jaraa'ed**	newspaper kiosk
ممنوع الدخول	**mamnooA ad-dokhool**	no entry
غرامة لسوء الاستخدام	**gharaamah li soo al-estekhdaam**	penalty for misuse
رصيف	**raseef**	platform
تذكرة رصيف	**tazkarat raseef**	platform ticket
طريق	**Tareeq**	road
حجز المقاعد	**Hajz al-maqaAed**	seat reservation
عربة نوم	**Arabat nawm**	sleeping car
مدخنون	**modakhenoon**	smokers
وجبات خفيفة	**wajabaat khafeefah**	snacks
شارع	**shaareA**	street
تكملة	**takmelah**	supplement

→

39

تذاكر / مكتب حجز التذاكر	taz**aa**ker/ m**a**ktab Hajz at-taz**aa**ker	tickets/ticket office
مكتب التذاكر	m**a**ktab at-taz**aa**ker	ticket office
جدول المواعيد	j**a**dwal al-mawa**ʌee**d	timetable
إلى القطارات	**e**la al-qeT**aa**r**a**t	to the trains
خالٍ	kh**aa**lee	vacant
غرفة الانتظار	gh**o**rfat al-entez**aa**r	waiting room

Things You'll Hear

enteb**aa**h
Attention

at-taz**aa**ker law sam**a**Ht
Tickets, please

AIR TRAVEL

All Arab countries have air links with the outside world. Many of the larger countries, particularly Saudi Arabia, have an efficient and modern internal service. As most travellers will arrive in their country of destination by air here is the place to give a word of warning: almost all Arab states have strict visa requirements for passport-holders from European and North American countries as well as Australia and New Zealand, and visas must very often be obtained from that country's embassy or consulate in the traveller's country of residence. Travellers without the correct visa may be refused entry. It is better not to travel to any Arab country other than Egypt with a passport containing Israeli stamps. Some countries, such as Saudi Arabia, will confiscate any alcohol or unsuitable literature you may be carrying, and the penalties for smuggling any types of illicit drugs are among the heaviest in the world. Arab police are particularly sensitive about 'plane spotters' and anyone photographing airports and aircraft. So use your common sense and don't risk being branded a spy.

USEFUL WORDS AND PHRASES

aircraft	Tayaarah
air hostess	moDeefah jaweeyah
airline	khaT Tayaraan
airport	maTaar
airport bus	baas al-maTaar
aisle	mamsha yafsel bayn al-karaasee
arrival	wosool
baggage claim	istilam al-Haqaa'eb
boarding card	beTaaqat as-soaood leT-Taa'erah
check-in	at-tasjeel wa ad-dokhool
check-in desk	maktab tasjeel wa dokhool ar-rokaab

customs	jomrok
delay	ta'akheer
departure	raHeel
departure lounge	qaAt ar-raHeel
emergency exit	makhraj aT-Tawaare'
flight	reHlah
flight number	raqam ar-reHlah
gate	bawaabah
jet	jet
to land	yahboT
long-distance flight	reHlat Tayaraan le-masaafah Taweelah
passport	jawaaz safar
passport control	moraaqabat al-jawaazaat
pilot	Tayaar
runway	madraj aT-Taa'eraat
seat	maqAd
seat belt	Hezaam al-maqAd
steward	moDeef
stewardess	moDeefah
takeoff	eqlaA
visa	veeza
window	shobaak
wing	janaaH

When is there a flight to …?
emta be-yakoon fee reHlat Tayaraan le …?

What time does the flight to … leave?
emta mawaed eqlaA Tayaarat …?

Is it a direct flight?
hal heya reHlah mobaasherah?

Do I have to change planes?
hal laazem oghayyer aT-Tayaarah?

When do I have to check in?
emta be-yakoon fee tasjeel ar-rokaab?

I'd like a single ticket to …
oreed tazkarat zehaab le …

I'd like a return ticket to …
oreed tazkarat zehaab wa Awdah le …

I'd like a non-smoking seat, please
oreed maqAd feel-joz' elee mamnooA feehee at-tadkheen
   law samaнt

I'd like a window seat, please
oreed maqAd janb ash-shobaak law samaнt

How long will the flight be delayed?
kam modat ta'akheer ar-reнlah?

Is this the right gate for the … flight?
hal haza al-bawaabah as-saнeeнah le-reнlat …?

Which gate for the flight to …?
ay bawaabah le-reнlat …?

When do we arrive in …?
emta nasel le …?

May I smoke now?
momken odakhen seejaarah al-нeen?

I don't feel very well
ana mareeD shway

THINGS YOU'LL SEE

طيارة	TayAArah	aircraft
وصول	wosool	arrivals
استلام الحقائب	istilam al-Haqaa'eb	baggage claim
تسجيل الركاب	tasjeel ar-rokaab	check-in
يسجل	yesajjil	to check in
جمارك	jamaarek	customs
مراقبة الجمارك	moraaqabat al-jamaarek	customs control
تأخير	ta'akheer	delay
رحيل	raHeel	departures
رحلة مباشرة	reHlah mobaasherah	direct flight
مخرج الطوارئ	makhraj aT-TawAAree'	emergency exit
هبوط إضطراري	hoboot eDTerAAree	emergency landing
اربط أحزمة المقاعد	erboT aHzemat al-maqaAed	fasten seat belt
رحلة	reHlah	flight
بوابة	bawAAbah	gate
معلومات	maAloomaat	information
هبوط	hoboot	landing
التوقيت المحلي	at-tawqeet al-maHalee	local time

→

44

لغير المدخنين	le-ghayr al-modakheneen	non-smokers
الرجاء الامتناع عن التدخين	ar-rejaa' al-emtenaA An at-tadkheen	no smoking, please
ركاب	rokaab	passengers
مراقبة جوازات السفر	moraaqabat jawaazaat as-safar	passport control
مدرج الطائرات	madraj aT-Taa'eraat	runway
رحلة محددة المواعيد	reHlah moHaddadat al-mawaaeed	scheduled flight
إقلاع	eqlaA	takeoff

THINGS YOU'LL HEAR

yasAd ar-rokaab al-aan ela aT-Taa'erah al-motajehah ela ...
The flight for ... is now boarding

ar-rejaa' at-tawajoh al-aan ela bawaabah raqam ...
Please go now to gate number ...

45

BY BUS AND TAXI

Bus travel is the main way Arabs get around their countries. In the almost complete absence of regular, fast rail services (see Rail Travel page 34 for exceptions) cities and towns are linked by regular, usually fast, bus services. Inter-city buses are almost without exception air-conditioned. If the route crosses any desert area, then there will definitely be air conditioning. Although you can usually buy your ticket as you board the bus, you can also buy it at the bus station and this is preferable since it can be done in a more leisurely and accurate way than in a jostling queue pushing to get aboard.

Within the large towns and cities the Westerner may find the buses very overcrowded and slow. Taxi travel may be preferred – they are relatively cheap. There are two types of taxi. One is just as in the West. But although these taxis do sometimes have meters the fare they show is not binding and a prospective passenger is wise to get a firm price out of the driver before setting off.

The other type of taxi is one which plies a fixed route and which can be shared by several passengers getting on and off at different points. These are called **taaksee servees**. Using these taxis, however, presupposes that you know where the cab is going. Since they do not carry any signs, only experience of a particular city will tell you this. These taxis are best used only by travellers who have an Arabic-speaking companion with them or by those who have an adventurous streak in them!

USEFUL WORDS AND PHRASES

adult	baalegh
boat	markeb
bus	baas
bus stop	maнaттat baasaat
child	тefl
coach	baas
conductor	moнassel tazaaker

connection	tawseelah
cruise	jawlah baHareeyah
driver	saa'eq
fare	ojrah
ferry	Abaarah
network map	khareeTat al-baasaat
number 5 bus	baas raqam khamsah
passenger	raakeb
port	meenaa'
quay	raseef al-meenaa'
river	nahr
seat	maqAd
station	maHaTTah
subway	nafaq
taxi	taaksee
terminus	maHaTTah nehaa'eeyah
ticket	tazkarah
tram	traam

Where is the bus station?
wayn maHaTTat al-baasaat?

Where is there a bus stop?
wayn maHaTTat baasaat qareebah?

Which buses go to ...?
aysh heya al-baasaat elee tarooH le ...?

How often do the buses to ... run?
kol qad aysh taseer al-baasaat elee raayeHah ela ...?

Would you tell me when we get to ...?
momken tonabehnee lama nasel ela ...?

Do I have to get off yet?
hal laazem anzel al-aan?

How do you get to …?
kayf tar<u>oo</u>H le …?

Is it very far?
hal h<u>e</u>ya ba<u>Aee</u>dah?

I want to go to …
or<u>ee</u>d ar<u>oo</u>h le …

Do you go near …?
hal tas<u>ee</u>r bel-q<u>o</u>rb men …?

Where can I buy a ticket?
men wayn asht<u>a</u>ree tazk<u>a</u>rah?

Do we have to pay for the children?
l<u>aa</u>zim n<u>i</u>dfA lil-aTf<u>aa</u>l?

Could you open/close the window?
m<u>o</u>mken t<u>e</u>ftah/t<u>a</u>qfel ash-shob<u>aa</u>k?

Could you help me get a ticket?
m<u>o</u>mken taq<u>oo</u>l lee kayf aj<u>ee</u>b tazk<u>a</u>rah?

When does the last bus leave?
<u>e</u>mta mee<u>A</u>ad qiy<u>aa</u>m <u>aa</u>kher ba<u>a</u>S?

How much will it cost?
qad aysh be-tatak<u>a</u>llef?

Is there are family ticket available?
hal fee tazk<u>a</u>rah lil-<u>Aa</u>'ilah?

Can you wait here and take me back?
m<u>o</u>mken tant<u>a</u>zer h<u>o</u>na wa teraja<u>A</u>nee m<u>a</u>rrah th<u>aa</u>nyah?

THINGS YOU'LL SEE

بالغون	baalegh<u>ee</u>n	adults
تكييف الهواء	taky<u>ee</u>f al-haw<u>aa</u>	air conditioning
يغير	yogh<u>a</u>yyer	to change
أطفال	aTf<u>aa</u>l	children
خروج	khor<u>oo</u>j	departure, exit
لا تتحدث مع السائق	laa tataH<u>a</u>ddath m<u>a</u>A as-s<u>aa</u>'eq	do not speak to the driver
مخرج الطوارئ	m<u>a</u>khraj aT-Taw<u>aa</u>ree'	emergency exit
مدخل	m<u>a</u>dkhal	entrance
الدخول من الأمام / الخلف	ad-dokh<u>oo</u>l men al-am<u>aa</u>m/ al-kh<u>a</u>lf	entry at the front/rear
كامل العدد	k<u>aa</u>mel al-<u>A</u>adad	full
ممنوع الدخول	mamn<u>oo</u>A ad-dokh<u>oo</u>l	no entry
ممنوع التدخين	mamn<u>oo</u>A at-tadkh<u>ee</u>n	no smoking
يدفع	y<u>a</u>dfaA	to pay
طريق	Tar<u>ee</u>q	route

$\longrightarrow$

49

مقاعد	**maqaAed**	seats
يعرض	**yaAreD**	to show
يقف	**yaqef**	stop
موقف التاكسيات	**mawqef at-taakseeyaat**	taxi rank
محطة نهائية	**moHaTTah nehaa'eeyah**	terminus
تذكرة	**tazkarah**	ticket

DOING BUSINESS

Western business travellers in the Arab world will find their counterparts both educated and sophisticated. Any idea that Arab business is carried out these days with the medieval conspiracies of the casbah must be utterly dismissed. Today's businessmen in every Arab country are part of the educated elite, often with ties to the political establishment in that country, which may control all major foreign trade dealings of that particular state. These businessmen will have considerable knowledge of Western ways and will often have travelled in Western countries themselves. An important point worth noting is that many businessmen in manufacturing industries in the Arab world are themselves engineers of high calibre and have great expertise in their product field. Western companies should ensure that a suitably qualified member of staff is despatched on business in areas requiring technical skill otherwise they may have rings drawn around them by their Arab hosts.

Arab hospitality is renowned throughout the world and rightly so. Westerners will find their Arab counterparts open and friendly, and genuine friendships will easily be made. Before any business meeting coffee or tea will be served, usually sweet and without milk and in very small cups. You may be offered two or three of these before finally beginning the business discussion.

You should always dress particularly neatly and always be on time for appointments. Men should wear a tie and short-sleeved shirt in hot climates, and a suit or jacket and tie in cooler environments. Women should wear long skirts or dresses and at least three-quarter length sleeves. You may well find that meetings and appointments do not run to a particularly punishing schedule and, indeed, you should allow for considerable delays in the timetable of events and plan your days accordingly, with room for rearrangement of dislocated events.

When you are introduced to Arab colleagues you should shake them by the hand. If you get to know someone well you may be embraced and even kissed and you should take this in your stride and reciprocate.

If you are invited out to dine with an Arab colleague you will usually be taken out to a restaurant – not to his home. The host always pays for everything and you should not even offer to pay. What you should do, however, is to extend your own invitation to your host to dine (at your expense!) in your hotel or a good restaurant you know.

Do not forget that in many Arab countries, particularly Saudi Arabia, alcohol is strictly forbidden. It is certainly frowned upon in most of the Arab world. While strong drink is often served in international hotels outside the peninsula, it is wise to refrain from drinking alcohol at all in the presence of Arab colleagues unless they make it clear they do not object. Your trip to the Arab world is the ideal time to clear your head and give your liver a break.

There are not very many businesswomen working as executives in Arab companies, although this is less true in certain areas such as arts and media. It is certainly true of Saudi Arabia, where women may not even drive a car or travel unescorted by a man, but applies to all Arab countries to a varying degree.

Useful Words and Phrases

accept	yaqbal
accountant	moHaaseb
accounts department	edaarat al-moHaasebah
advertisement	eAlaan
advertising	eAlaanaat
to airfreight	yashHen bel-jaw
bid	ATaa'
board (of directors)	hay'ah
brochure	kotayeb
business card	kaart

business person *(male)*	rajol aAmaal
(female)	sayyeedit aAmaal
chairperson *(male)*	ra'ees
(female)	ra'eesah
cheap	rakhees
client	Ameel
company	sherkah
computer	kompyooter
consumer	mostahlik
contract	Aqd
cost	taklefah
customer	zaboon
director	modeer
discount	takhfeeD
documents	wathaa'eq
down payment	Arboon
engineer	mohandes
executive	monaffez
expensive	ghaalee
exports	saaderaat
fax	faaks
to import	yastawred
imports	waaredaat
instalment	dofAh
invoice	faatoorah
to invoice	yorsel faatoorah le
letter	kheTaab
letter of credit	kheTaab eAtemaad
loss	khosaarah
manager	modeer
manufacture	sanAh
margin	rebH ejmaalee
market	sooq
marketing	tasweeq
meeting	ejtemaA
negotiations	mofaawaDaat

offer	ArD
order	Talab
to order	yaTlob
personnel	hay'at al-mowazafeen
price	seAr
product	montaj
production	entaaj
profit	rebн
promotion (*publicity*)	tarweej
purchase order	Talab sheraa'
sales department	qesm al-mabeeAat
sales director	modeer mabeeAat
sales figures	arqaam al-mabeeAat
secretary (*male*)	sekretayr
(*female*)	sekretayrah
shipment	shoннah
tax	Dareebah
tender	ATaa' fee monaaqasah
total	majmooA

My name is …
esmee …

Here's my card
tafaDal kaartee

Pleased to meet you
tasharafna be-moqaabelatak

May I introduce …?
momken oqadem lak …?

My company is …
sherkatee esmaha …

Our product is selling very well in the UK market
beDaAtna Alayha eqbaal shadeed fee aswaaq engeltera

We are looking for partners in the Arab world
neHna be-nabHath An shorakaa' feel-Aalem al-Arabee

At our last meeting …
fee moqaabelatna al-akheerah …

10%/25%/50%
Asharah feel-me'ah/khamsah wa Aeshreen feel-me'ah/khamseen feel-me'ah

More than …
akthar men …

Less than …
aqal men …

We're on schedule
neHna maasheeyeen Hasab al-jadwal tamaaman

We're slightly behind schedule
neHna mota'akhareen qaleelan

Please accept our apologies
arjook eqbaal eAtezaarna

There are good government grants available
fee menaH momtaazah men al-Hokoomah

It's a deal
mowaafeq

I'll have to check that with my chairman
laazem aakhoz ra'y al-modeer al-Aam

I'll get back to you on that
be-arod Alayk qareeban be-khosoos haza al-mawDOOA

Our quote will be with you very shortly
be-norsel lak as-seAr qareeban jedan

We'll send it by fax
sa-norselha bet-faaks

We'll send them airfreight
sa-noshHenha beT-Tayaarah

It's a pleasure to do business with you
yosaAednee an atAamel maAk

Can we invite you to dinner in our hotel?
momken nadAook lel-Ashaa' fee fondoqna?

We look forward to a mutually beneficial business relationship
atamana enha takoon Alaaqat Amal mofeedah leT-Tarafayn

EATING OUT

All large hotels have a restaurant which serves meals in the
Western style, although the menu will probably contain some
traditional Arab dishes and some specialities of the region you
are in. If you are staying at a smaller hotel without its own
restaurant you are sure to find a range of local restaurants
covering different price ranges. Restaurants often specialise in
dishes based on one type of food: lamb grills, fowl of various
kinds or perhaps fish and seafood.

Most Arab countries serve alcohol in tourist hotels but
some, such as Saudi Arabia, Qatar and the United Arab Emirates,
will not permit anyone to drink alcohol legally anywhere at
any time.

Arab cooking is mainly based on mutton, lamb, fish or chicken.
Pork is not eaten by Muslims and cooking in wine is very rare.

Restaurants are set out as they are in the West and, as well as
table napkins, they often provide finger-bowls. It is considered
impolite to smoke during a meal, even in between courses.
Several small cups of bitter coffee are served at the end of a meal.

Coffee in the Arab world normally means Turkish coffee, which
is taken very strong and black – like an espresso with cardamom
and other spices in it. You can have it three ways: no sugar –
saadah; medium – **mazbooт**; sweet – **sukkar zeyaadah**.

Apart from conventional Western-style restaurants you can
also eat out at a snack-bar (**kaafeterya**) where cheaper salad-
type dishes are served, often based on beans or spicy fried
chickpea balls.

In all major towns there will also be kiosks selling glasses of
fruit juice or canned drinks and biscuits and crisps.

USEFUL WORDS AND PHRASES

bottle	zojaajah
cake	kayk
coffee	qahwah
cup	fenjaan

fork	sh<u>a</u>wkah
glass	koob/koobayah
knife	sek<u>ee</u>n
menu	qaa'<u>e</u>mat aT-T Aam
milk	Hal<u>ee</u>b
plate	Tabaq/labad
sandwich	s<u>a</u>ndwetsh
serviette	f<u>oo</u>Tah lel-maa'edah
snack	w<u>a</u>jbah khaf<u>ee</u>fah
soup	sh<u>o</u>rbah
spoon	malAaqah
sugar	s<u>u</u>kkar
table	Taawlah
tea	sh<u>aa</u>y
tip	baqsh<u>ee</u>sh
water	miy<u>aa</u>h
white coffee	q<u>a</u>hwah bel-Hal<u>ee</u>b
wine	nab<u>ee</u>z
wine list	qaa'<u>e</u>mat an-nab<u>ee</u>z

A table for two, please
Taawlah le-shakhs<u>ay</u>n law s<u>a</u>m<u>a</u>Ht

Can I see the menu?
m<u>o</u>mken ash<u>oo</u>f qaa'<u>e</u>mat aT-Taam law sam<u>a</u>Ht?

What would you recommend?
t<u>a</u>wsee be-<u>ay</u> n<u>a</u>wA?

I'd like ...
or<u>ee</u>d ...

Just a cup of coffee, please
fenj<u>aa</u>n q<u>a</u>hwah f<u>a</u>qaT, law sam<u>a</u>Ht

Waiter/waitress!
ya gars<u>oo</u>n/ya gars<u>oo</u>nah!

Can we have the bill, please?
m<u>o</u>mken al-H<u>esaa</u>b, law sam<u>a</u>Ht?

Is there a set menu?
hal fee qaa'<u>e</u>mah moH<u>aa</u>dadah?

Do you do children's portions?
fee H<u>a</u>jm sagh<u>ee</u>r lil-aTf<u>aa</u>l?

Is this suitable for vegetarians?
hal h<u>a</u>za mun<u>aa</u>sib lil-nab<u>aa</u>tiyeen?

I didn't order this
<u>a</u>na ma T<u>a</u>l<u>a</u>bt h<u>a</u>za

May we have some more …?
m<u>o</u>mken shew<u>a</u>yah k<u>a</u>man … law sam<u>a</u>Ht?

The meal was very good, thank you
al-w<u>a</u>jbah k<u>aa</u>nat momt<u>aa</u>zah, sh<u>o</u>kran

---

YOU MAY HEAR

bel-han<u>aa</u>' wash-shef<u>aa</u>'!
Enjoy your meal!

YOU MAY SEE

مطعم   **maTAam**   restaurant

MENU GUIDE

STARTERS, SOUPS AND SALADS

سلاطة باذنجان	**salaaTat baazenjaan**	aubergine salad
بوريك	**booreek**	'bourek' – savoury pastry
كافيار	**kaafiyaar**	caviar
كبد دجاج (فراخ)	**kibd dajaaj (feraakh)**	chicken liver
شوربة دجاج	**shoorbat dajaaj**	chicken soup
شوربة صافية	**shorbah saafeeyah**	consommé
شوربة تبولة	**shorbat taboolah**	cracked wheat soup
فتة	**fattah**	festival soup – with lamb, rice and tomato
شوربة سمك	**shoorbat samak**	fish soup
عصير فاكهة	**Aseer faakehah**	fruit juice
حنود شامي	**Hanood shaamee**	garlic and rice salad
سلاطة خضراء	**salaaTah khaDra'**	green salad
حمص	**Hommos**	hummus – puréed chickpeas
شوربة عدس	**shoorbat Adas**	lentil soup
شمام	**shammaam**	melon

زيتون	zayt<u>oo</u>n	olives
سلاطة شرقية	sal<u>aa</u>tah sharq<u>ee</u>yah	Oriental mixed, vegetable salad
باتيه	paat<u>ee</u>h	pâté
مخللات	mekhallal<u>aa</u>t	pickles
سلاطة بطاطس	sal<u>aa</u>тat baт<u>aa</u>тes	potato salad
سلاطة	sal<u>aa</u>тah	salad
سردين	sard<u>ee</u>n	sardines
شوربة	sh<u>oo</u>rbah	soup
مزة	m<u>a</u>zzah	starter
ورق عنب محشي	w<u>a</u>raq ʌ<u>e</u>nab m<u>a</u>Hshee	stuffed vine leaves
تبولة	tab<u>oo</u>lah	'taboola' – cracked wheat
طحينة	тaн<u>ee</u>nah	'tahina' – sesame seed paste
بابا غنوج	b<u>aa</u>ba ghan<u>oo</u>j	'tahina' with aubergine
سلاطة طماطم	sal<u>aa</u>тat тam<u>aa</u>тem	tomato salad
ملوخية	molookh<u>ee</u>yah	traditional soup of garlic and greens
شوربة خضار	sh<u>oo</u>rbat khoᴅ<u>aa</u>r	vegetable soup
سلاطة جرجير	sal<u>aa</u>тat jarj<u>ee</u>r	watercress salad
سلاطة خيار باللبن	sal<u>aa</u>тat khiy<u>aa</u>r bel-l<u>a</u>ban	yoghurt and cucumber salad

EGGS, CHEESE AND PASTA

بيضة مسلوقة	**bay**Dah masl**oo**qah	boiled egg
جبنة	j**e**bnah	cheese
لبنة	l**a**bnah	curd cheese
بيضة	**bay**Dah	egg
مش	**mesh**	firm, salty cheese
بيضة مقلية	**bay**Dah maql**ee**yah	fried egg
جبنة رومي	j**e**bnah r**oo**mee	hard cheese
مكرونة	makar**oo**nah	macaroni
كوسة بجبنة	k**oo**sah be-j**e**bnah	marrow and cheese dish
جبنة قديمة	j**e**bnah qad**ee**mah	mature cheese
شعرية	she**A**r**ee**yah	noodles
عجة	**A**ejah	omelette with onions and parsley
جبنة مالحة	j**e**bnah maal**e**Hah	salty cheese
شكشوكة	shaksh**oo**kah	scrambled eggs with mince
جبنة فلاحي	j**e**bnah falaa**Hee**	soft cheese
مكرونة سباجيتي	makar**oo**nah spagh**e**tti	spaghetti
جبنة بيضاء	j**e**bnah **bay**Da'	white cheese

FISH

أنشوجة	**anshoogah**	anchovies
شبوط	**shaboot**	carp
كافيار	**kaafiyaar**	caviar
كابوريا	**kaabooriya**	crab
ثعابين الماء	**thaaabeen al-maa'**	eels
سمك	**samak**	fish
برشات سمك	**taraushaat samak**	fish fillets
سمك بزيت	**samak be-zayt**	fish in oil
سمك طرطور	**samak тartoor**	fish with garlic sauce
سمك صيادية	**samak sayaadeeyah**	fish with rice
سمك مقلٍ	**samak maqlee**	fried fish
سمك مشوٍ	**samak mashwee**	grilled fish
كركند	**kerkend**	lobster
استاكوزا	**estakooza**	(in Egypt) lobster
بوري	**booree**	mullet
اخطبوط	**akhтaboot**	octopus
محار	**maнaar**	oysters
فرخ	**farkh**	perch
جمبري	**jambaree**	prawns
سردين	**sardeen**	sardines
سمك مدخن	**samak medakhan**	smoked fish
سمك موسى	**samak moosa**	sole

حبار	Habaar	squid
سمك الأطروط	samak al-aTroot	trout
تونة	toonah	tuna
سمك الترس	samak at-ters	turbot

MEAT AND FOWL

لحم بقري	laHm baqaree	beef
بفتيك	boftayk	beefsteak
صدر	sadr	breast
فراخ / دجاج	firaakh/dajaaj	chicken
كفتة دجاج	koftat dajaaj	chicken balls
كستليتة	kosteleetah	cutlet
بط	baTT	duck
اسكالوب	eskaaloob	escalope
فيليتو	feelett	fillet
وز	wezz	goose
كباب	kebaab	grilled lamb on a skewer
حمام مشوٍ	Hamaam mashwee	grilled pigeon
كلاوي	kalaawee	kidneys
لحم ضاني	laHm Daanee	lamb
ريش ضاني	reeyash Daanee	lamb chop
ورك	werk	leg
فخذ ضاني	fakhz Daanee	leg of lamb

كبدة	**kebdah**	liver
لحم	**laHm**	meat
كفتة	**koftah**	meatballs
لحم مفروم	**laHm mafroom**	minced meat
لحوم مشوية	**luHoom mashweeyah**	mixed grilled meats
حمام	**Hamaam**	pigeon
أرنب	**arnab**	rabbit
روسبيف	**roosbeef**	roast beef
دجاج في الفرن	**dajaaj feel-forn**	roast chicken
ضاني في الفرن	**Daannee feel-forn**	roast lamb on a spit
كتف ضاني	**ketef Daannee**	shoulder of lamb
شاورمة	**shaawerma**	sliced spit-roast lamb/ chicken
سجق حار	**sojoq Haar**	spicy salami
لحم أوزي	**laHm oozee**	spring lamb
ضاني مسلوق	**Daanee maslooq**	steamed lamb
طاجن بتلو	**Taajen betello**	substantial veal stew
لسان	**lesaan**	tongue
ديك رومي	**deek roomee**	turkey
سجق	**sojoq**	type of sausage
بتلو	**betello**	veal
اسكالوب بتلو	**eskaloob betello**	veal escalope

MAIN DISHES

مسقعة	**mosaqqAh**	aubergine with raisins and meat
حمام بالفريك	**Hamaam bel-fereek**	chicken served with hard-boiled eggs
فراخ شركسية	**feraakh sharkaseeyah**	chicken with rice, chilli and nuts
كشك بالفراخ	**keshk bel-feraakh**	chicken with yoghurt and onion
كسكس بالضاني	**koos-koos be-Daanee**	couscous – lamb and steamed semolina
كباب سمك	**kebaab samak**	grilled fish on a skewer with tomatoes and green peppers
فلافل	**falaafel**	falafel – fried balls of ground beans or chickpeas
طعمية	**TAAmeeyah**	fried balls of ground beans with herbs
كشري	**kosharee**	'kosharee' – mixed rice, lentils, pasta and onions in a piquant sauce
لحم ضاني برياني	**laHm Daanee bereeyaanee**	lamb biriyani
مقلوبة	**maqloobah**	meat stewed with aubergines and rice

كفتة مبرومة	koftah mobroomah	minced meat with nuts
قدرة فراخ	qedrat feraakh	North African chicken stew
صفيحة	safeeHah	pastry base topped with minced lamb
لسان العصفور	lesaan al-Aosfoor	stewed lamb with vermicelli
دفينة	dafeenah	thick stew of chickpeas and beans

VEGETABLES

خرشوف	kharshoof	artichokes
الهليون	al-helyoon	asparagus
باذنجان	baazenjaan	aubergine
أبوكادو	abookaado	avocado
فول مهروس	fool mahroos	bean purée
بنجر	banjar	beetroot
فول أخضر	fool akhDar	broad beans
كرنب	koronb	cabbage
جزر	jazar	carrots
أرنبيط	arnabeeт	cauliflower
كرفس	karafs	celery
فلفل حامي	felfel Haamee	chillies
كوسة	koosah	courgettes

خيار	**khiy<u>aa</u>r**	cucumber
ثوم	**thoom**	garlic
فاصوليا خضراء	**fas<u>oo</u>liya kh<u>a</u>ᴅra'**	green beans
فاصوليا خضراء بزيت	**fas<u>oo</u>liya kh<u>a</u>ᴅra' be-z<u>ay</u>t**	green beans cooked in oil
فلفل أخضر	**f<u>e</u>lfel <u>a</u>khᴅar**	green peppers
فاصوليا	**fas<u>oo</u>liya**	haricot beans
طرطوفة	**ᴛarᴛ<u>oo</u>fah**	Jerusalem artichokes
كراث	**kor<u>aa</u>th**	leeks
عدس	**<u>A</u>das**	lentils
خس	**khass**	lettuce
باذنجان مخلل	**bazenj<u>aa</u>n mekh<u>a</u>llel**	marinated aubergine
بامية	**b<u>aa</u>myah**	okra, ladies' fingers
بصل	**b<u>a</u>sal**	onions
بازلاء	**baaz<u>e</u>lla**	peas
بطاطس	**baᴛ<u>aa</u>ᴛes**	potatoes
فجل	**f<u>e</u>jel**	radishes
رز	**rozz**	rice
سبانخ	**sab<u>aa</u>nekh**	spinach
بصل أخضر	**b<u>a</u>sal <u>a</u>khᴅar**	spring onions
كرنب محشٍ	**kor<u>o</u>nb m<u>a</u>ʜshee**	stuffed cabbage
فلفل محشٍ	**f<u>e</u>lfel m<u>a</u>ʜshee**	stuffed peppers

بطاطس محشية	baTaaTes maHsheeyah	stuffed potatoes
ذرة	zorrah	sweet corn
بطاطا	baTaaTaa	sweet potatoes
طماطم	TamaaTem	tomatoes
لفت	left	turnips
خضار	khoDaar	vegetables
جرجير	jarjeer	watercress

FRUIT AND NUTS

لوز	looz	almonds
تفاح	teffaaH	apples
مشمش	meshmesh	apricots
موز	mooz	bananas
توت عليق	toot Aleeq	blackberries
الكستناء	al-kestenaa'	chestnuts
جوز الهند	jooz al-hend	coconut
فواكه مجففة	fawaakeh mojaffafah	dried fruit
محمصات	moHammasaat	dried seeds
تين	teen	figs
فواكه	fawaakeh	fruit
جريب فروت	grayb froot	grapefruit
عنب	Aenab	grapes
بندق	bondoq	hazelnuts
ليمون حامض	laymoon HaameD	lemon

ليمون	**laymoon**	limes
مانجة	**maanjah**	mangoes
شمام	**shammaam**	melon
جوز	**jooz**	nuts
برتقال	**bortogaal**	oranges
خوخ	**khookh**	peaches
فول سوداني	**fool soodaanee**	peanuts
كمثرى	**komethra**	pears
أناناس	**annaanaas**	pineapple
فستق	**fostoq**	pistachio nuts
برقوق	**barqooq**	plums
زبيب	**zebeeb**	raisins
راوند	**rawand**	rhubarb
فراولة	**farawlah**	strawberries
يسفندي	**yoosefendee**	tangerines
بطيخ	**bateekh**	watermelon

DESSERTS

سنبوسك باللوز	**senboosak bel-looz**	almond slice
بسكويت	**baskooweet**	biscuits
كيك	**kayk**	cake
كريم كراميل	**kreem karamel**	crème caramel

بلح الشام	**balaн ash-shaam**	'Dates of Damascus' – fried tartlets with syrup
حلويات	**наlawiyaat**	dessert
رز بلبن	**rozz be-laban**	dish of rice with milk and rosewater
خشاف	**khoshaaf**	dish of stewed fruits
كل واشكر	**kol wa oshkor**	'Eat and be Thankful' – little cake with layered pastry, nuts and syrup
بقلاوة	**baqlaawah**	fine layered pastry and nuts in syrup
زلابية	**zalaabeeyah**	fritters coated in syrup
سلاطة فواكه	**salaatet fawaakeh**	fruit salad
عسل النحل	**Asal an-naнl**	honey
آيس كريم	**aays kreem**	ice cream
صرة الست	**sorat as-sett**	'Lady's Navel' – type of doughnut with syrup
بلوظة	**baloozah**	milk pudding
أم علي	**omm Alee**	'Mother of Ali' – pudding with raisins and milk
كنافة	**konaafah**	pastry with nuts and syrup
رز بلبن	**rozz be-laban**	rice pudding

بسيمة	**baseemah**	semolina and coconut pudding
بسبوسة	**basboosah**	semolina cake with syrup
معمول	**maAmool**	small stuffed cake
قشطة	**qeshTah**	thick cream
ملبن	**malban**	Turkish Delight

DRINKS

سفن أب	**seven-up**	7-up®
بيرة	**beerah**	beer
بيرة معلبة	**beerah moAllabah**	canned beer
قهوة كابتشينو	**qahwah kaapetsheeno**	cappuccino
عصير جزر	**Aseer jazar**	carrot juice
شكولاتة	**shokoolaatah**	chocolate
كوكاكولا	**coca cola**	Coca Cola®
قهوة	**qahwah**	coffee
قهوة بحليب	**qahwah be-Haleeb**	coffee with milk
قهوة سادة	**qahwah saada**	coffee without sugar
قهوة أكسبرسو	**qahwah ekspresso**	espresso coffee
جن	**jenn**	gin
عصير عنب	**Aseer Aenab**	grape juice

بيرة ستلا	**b<u>ee</u>rah st<u>e</u>lla**	lager
عصير ليمون	**As<u>ee</u>r laym<u>oo</u>n**	lemon juice
شاي بليمون	**shaay be-laym<u>oo</u>n**	lemon tea
ملكشيك	**m<u>e</u>lkshayk**	milkshake
مياه معدنية	**miy<u>aa</u>h ma<u>A</u>dan<u>ee</u>yah**	mineral water
نعناع	**ne<u>A</u>n<u>a</u>A**	mint
عصير برتقال	**As<u>ee</u>r bortog<u>aa</u>l**	orange juice
بيبسي كولا	**p<u>e</u>psi c<u>o</u>la**	Pepsi®
صودا	**s<u>oo</u>da**	soda water
شاي	**shaay**	tea
شاي بحليب	**shaay be-H<u>a</u>l<u>ee</u>b**	tea with milk
شاي بدون سكر	**shaay be-d<u>oo</u>n s<u>o</u>kkar**	tea without sugar
تونيك	**t<u>oo</u>neek**	tonic water
قهوة تركي	**q<u>a</u>hwah t<u>o</u>rkee**	Turkish coffee
ماء	**maa'**	water
ويسكي	**w<u>ee</u>skee**	whisky
نبيذ	**nab<u>ee</u>z**	wine

BASIC FOODS

زبدة	**z<u>e</u>bdah**	butter
قهوة	**q<u>a</u>hwah**	coffee
دقيق	**daq<u>ee</u>q**	flour

أعشاب	**aashaab**	herbs
مربى	**merabba**	jam
مرجرين	**marjereen**	margarine
حليب	**Haleeb**	milk
مستردة	**mastardah**	mustard
زيت	**zayt**	oil
فلفل أسود	**felfel aswad**	pepper
ملح	**melH**	salt
سكر	**sokkar**	sugar
شاي	**shaay**	tea
خل	**khall**	vinegar
ماء	**maa'**	water
زبادي	**zabaadee**	yoghurt

TYPES OF BREAD

سميط	**semeeT**	bagels
خبز	**khobz**	bread
خبز بلدي	**khobz baladee**	large thin flat brown bread
سندوتش	**sandwetsh**	sandwich
فينو	**feenoo**	white bread rolls
خبز شامي	**khobz shaamee**	white pitta bread

CULINARY METHODS OF PREPARATION

في الفرن	**feel-f<u>o</u>rn**	baked
مشوٍ على الفحم	**m<u>a</u>shwee <u>A</u>la al-f<u>a</u>Hm**	barbecued
مسلوق	**masl<u>oo</u>q**	boiled
مقلٍ	**m<u>a</u>qlee**	fried
مشوٍ	**m<u>a</u>shwee**	grilled
في الفرن	**feel-f<u>o</u>rn**	roasted
متبل	**mct<u>a</u>bbel**	spiced
مسبك	**mes<u>a</u>bbek**	stewed
محشٍ	**m<u>a</u>Hshee**	stuffed

SHOPPING

The sheer size and variety of the Arab world, some twenty diverse countries, precludes here anything other than general statements about shopping. In broad terms, however, the great majority of shops of any size, department stores and government offices are closed all day on Fridays, which is the Muslim day of rest and worship in the mosques. The exceptions are barbers and hairdressers who are open on Fridays, when people can get to them easily, but stay closed on Mondays instead.

Shops and offices usually open on other days from about 10 am until 1 pm, when they close for siesta, and reopen at around 4 pm and finally close at 7 pm. In this way traders, merchants and civil servants do not have to work in the often suffocating heat of the afternoon.

The tourist and businessman alike are usually drawn not to department stores but to the Arab bazaar, souk or casbah; it is given a different name in every city. This is usually to be found in the oldest part of the city and has often kept much the same form for centuries, with narrow winding streets and alleyways lined with many little shops and stalls. Similar goods will generally be grouped in the same area, so there will be a spice section, a clothes section and so on. If you are a romantic at heart then this the place for you – where the *Tales from the Thousand and One Nights* come to life.

One thing which is often a new experience for the Western visitor to the bazaar is the age-old custom of bargaining for goods, especially ornamental and artistic wares. Larger shops display prices for the goods just as in the West. Many people are timid about enquiring about the prices of goods in the bazaar but the simple rule is this: when the salesman gives a price, offer him half what he is asking and wait for his reaction. Accompany this low bid with the words **yeftah allah** – this will avoid any offence being taken. He may well then offer the goods at a different price and you could well halve the difference again and, in all probability, walk off with the goods at a sensible price. Naturally, every case should be treated on its merits and you should also bear in mind what you consider a fair price regardless of the terms being offered.

Apart from thousands of different types of chess-boards, samovars and rugs the best value to be had, in real terms, is from the gold and silversmiths. Precious metals are sold by weight, not design, and there are some real bargains to be had in this area. Obviously this is one field where the scope for haggling is circumscribed but, compared to the West, prices are very favourable anyway.

USEFUL WORDS AND PHRASES

audio equipment	moAedaat sawteeyah
baker	khabaaz
butcher	jazaar
bookshop	maktabah
to buy	yashtaree
cake shop	Halawaanee
cheap	rakhees
chemist	saydaleeyah
department store	dokaan kabeer/maHall kabeer
fashion	azaa'
fishmonger	baa'eA as-samak
florist	dokaan zohoor
goldsmith	saa'egh
grocer	baqaal
ironmonger	taajer Hadaa'ed
menswear	malaabes rejaal
newsagent	dokaan jaraa'ed wa soHof
receipt	wasl
record and cassette shop	dokaan estewaanaat wa ashretat tasjeel
rug	sejaadah
sale	ookazeeyoon
samovar	samaawar
shoe shop	dokaan aHzeeyah

shop	dokaan
silversmith	saa'egh al-feDDah
to go shopping	yatasawwaq
souvenir shop	dokaan al-hadaaya at-tezkaareeyah
special offer	ARD khaas
to spend	yasrof
stationer	dokaan al-adawaat al-maktabeeyah
supermarket	soopermaarket
tailor	khayaaT
till	khazeenah
toyshop	dokaan leAb aTfaal
travel agent	maktab safareeyaat
women's wear	malaabes nesaa'

I'd like …
oreed …

Do you have …?
hal Andak …?

How much is this?
be-kam haza?

That's too much
haza ghaalee jeddan

I'll give you …
be-aATeek …

That's my best offer
haza aHsan seAr

Two for …
ethnayn be …

OK, I'll take it
zayn, be-ashtareeha

Where is the … department?
wayn qesm al-…?

Do you have any more of these?
hal Andak al-mazeed men haadool?

I'd like to change this, please
oreed oghayyer haza law samaHt

Have you anything cheaper?
hal Andak ay shay' arkhas?

Have you anything larger?
hal Andak ay shay' akbar?

Have you anything smaller?
hal Andak ay shay' asghar?

Does it come in other colours?
Andak alwaan thaaneeyah?

Could you wrap it for me?
momken taleffha law samaHt?

Can I have a receipt?
momken faatoorah law samaHt?

Can I have a bag, please?
momken kees law samaHt?

Can I try it/them on?
momken ojarrebha?

Where do I pay?
wayn <u>a</u>dfaA?

Can I have a refund?
m<u>o</u>mken or<u>a</u>jeA h<u>a</u>za wa astar<u>e</u>d qeem<u>a</u>t-ho?

I'm just looking
<u>a</u>na be-<u>aa</u>khoz f<u>e</u>krah f<u>a</u>qaT

I'll come back later
<u>a</u>na be-<u>a</u>rjaA baAd<u>a</u>yn

THINGS YOU'LL SEE

مخبز	m<u>a</u>khbaz	bakery
صفقة	s<u>a</u>fqah	bargain
بازار	baz<u>aar</u>	bazaar
مكتبة	makt<u>a</u>bah	bookshop
جزار	jazz<u>aar</u>	butcher
حلواني	Halaw<u>aa</u>nee	cake shop
قصبة	q<u>a</u>sbah	casbah
رخيص	rakh<u>ee</u>s	cheap
قسم	qesm	department
محل كبير	maH<u>a</u>ll kab<u>ee</u>r	department store
أزياء	azy<u>aa</u>'	fashion
زهور	zoh<u>oo</u>r	flowers
بقالة	beq<u>aa</u>lah	groceries

→

محل آيس كريم	ma<u>H</u>all ays kreem	ice cream shop
مواد لتنظيف المنزل	maw<u>aa</u>d le-tan<u>z</u>eef al-m<u>a</u>nzel	household cleaning materials
الطابق الأرضي	aT-T<u>aa</u>beq al-<u>a</u>rDee	lower floor
سوق	sooq	market, bazaar
ملابس رجال	mal<u>aa</u>be<u>s</u> rej<u>aa</u>l	menswear
محل بيع الأدوات المكتبية	ma<u>H</u>all bayA al-maktab<u>ee</u>yah	office supplies
الرجاء عدم اللمس	ar-rej<u>aa</u>' Adam al-l<u>a</u>ms	please do not touch
الرجاء أخذ عربة / سلة	ar-rej<u>aa</u>' akhz Arabah/s<u>a</u>llah	please take a trolley/basket
سعر	s<u>e</u>Ar	price
مخفض	mokh<u>a</u>ffaD	reduced
إيجار	eej<u>aa</u>r	rental
اخدم نفسك	<u>e</u>khdem n<u>a</u>fsak	self-service
محل أحذية	ma<u>H</u>all <u>a</u>Hzeayah	shoe shop
عرض خاص	ArD khaas	special offer
أوكازيون الصيف	awk<u>aa</u>zeay<u>oo</u>n as-s<u>a</u>yf	summer sale
محل سجاير	ma<u>H</u>all sej<u>aa</u>yer	tobacconist
لعب	leAb	toys
مكتب سفريات	m<u>a</u>ktab safarey<u>aa</u>t	travel agent

→

81

الطابق العلوي	aT-Taabeq al-Aolwee	upper floor
خضروات	khaDrawaat	vegetables
لا نستطيع إعطاء رد قيمة نقدي	laa nastaTeeA eATaa' radd qeemah naqdee	we cannot give cash refunds
ملابس نساء	malaabes nesaa'	women's clothing
قسم السيدات	qesm as-sayedaat	women's department

THINGS YOU'LL HEAR

ahlan wasahlan, ay khedmah?
Are you being served?

hal Andak khordah/fakkah?
Have you any smaller money/change?

ana aasef ma Andana ay makhzoon men haza an-nawA
I'm sorry, we're out of stock

haza kol ma howa Andana
This is all we have

ay khedmah thaaneeyah?
Will there be anything else?

POST OFFICES AND BANKS

In general terms, post offices in the Arab world open every day (with the exception of Friday) between approximately 8.30 am and 12 noon, and often open again in the late afternoon and evening between 4.30 and 7.30. Many of them close on Sunday afternoons. All are open on Saturdays.

They have these opening times in common with government offices and many shops. Post offices are mainly used for sending mail, although you can often make a local telephone call from a post office (see Telephones page 88). Since some Arab countries do not have a regular door-to-door delivery service for mail, the post office usually has a large poste restante section. If you are going to be settled in a particular place for more than a month or so you may consider opening a P.O. Box yourself.

Banks are normally open in the morning during the same hours as post offices – although some will re-open in the afternoon – and you can usually change foreign currency into local currency, although not necessarily the other way round. Often the only place where you can change local currency into foreign convertible currency will be in a large international hotel, a large bank or at an international airport. It is a golden rule when travelling off the beaten track not to acquire any more local currency than you actually require, as you may find it impossible to re-exchange it when you leave.

Each Arab state has its own national currency and although several are called 'riyals' or 'dinars' they each have a different value, depending on the country. A list of the current value of each currency is available in newspapers or on-line services.

Currencies in use across the Arab world are listed below:

Algeria	Dinar
Bahrain	Dinar
Egypt	Egyptian Pound (Gunayh)
the Emirates	Dirham
Iraq	Iraqi Dinar
Jordan	Jordanian Dinar

Kuwait	Kuwaiti Dinar
Lebanon	Lebanese Pound
Libya	Libyan Dinar
Mauritania	Ouguiya
Morocco	Dirham
North Yemen	Riyal
Oman	Omani Riyal
Qatar	Riyal
Saudi Arabia	Riyal
Somalia	Shilling
South Yemen	Dinar
Sudan	Pound
Syria	Syrian Pound
Tunisia	Dinar

USEFUL WORDS AND PHRASES

airmail	bareed jawee
bank	bank
banknotes	al-awraaq an-naqdeeyah
to change	yoHawwel
cheque	sheek
collection	taHseel
counter	kaawnter
customs form	estemaarat al-jomrok
delivery	tasleem
deposit	Arboon
exchange rate	seAr at-taghyeer
fax	faaks
form	estemaarah
international	Hewaalah maaleeyah
money order	doowaleeyah
letter	kheTaab/risalah
letter box	sondooq boosTah
mail	bareed
money order	Hewaalah maaleeyah
package, parcel	Tard

P.O. Box	sandooq bareed
post	boostah
postage rates	rosoom al-bareed
postal order	Hewaalah bareedeeyah
postcard	beTaaqah bareedeeyah
postcode	ramz bareedee
poste restante	yoHfaz be-maktab al-bareed
postman	boosTajee
post office	maktab al-bareed
pound	jenayh
pound sterling	jenayh esterleenee
registered letter	kheTaab mosajjal
stamp	TaabeA bareed
surface mail	al-bareed al-Aadee
traveller's cheque	sheek siyaaHee

How much is a letter/postcard to ...?
be-kam ersaal al-kheTaab/beTaaqah bareedeeyah ela ...?

I would like a stamp for a postcard to England
oreed ashtaree TaabeA le-enkeltera

I want to register this letter
oreed orsel haza al-jawaab mosajjal

I want to send this parcel to ...
oreed orsel haza aT-Tard ela ...

Where can I post this?
wayn aDaA haza al-kheTaab le-ersaalho bel-bareed?

Is there any mail for me?
hal fee ay kheTaabaat lee?

This is to go airmail
erselha bel-bareed al-jawee

I'd like to change this into …
oreed oghayyer haza ela …

Can I cash these traveller's cheques?
momken aqboD thaman hazehe ash-sheekaat as-siyaaHeeyah?

What is the exchange rate for the pound?
ma howa seAr at-taghyeer lel-jenayh?

THINGS YOU'LL SEE

عنوان	Aonwaan	address
المرسل إليه	al-morsal elayhee	addressee
بريد جوي	bareed jawee	airmail
بنك	bank	bank
مكتب الصرافة	maktab as-seraafah	bureau de change
أوقات جمع الرسائل	awqaat jamA ar-rasaa'el	collection times
رسم	rasm	charge
مستعجل	mestaAjel	express
بريد داخلي	bareed daakhelee	inland postage
خطاب	kheTaab	letter
صندوق بريد	sondooq bareed	letter box
حوالات نقدية	Hewaalaat naqdeeyah	money orders
مواعيد العمل	mowaaAeed al-Amal	opening hours
طرد	Tard	packet

→

كاونتر الطرود	kaawnter aT-Torood	parcels counter
رسوم البريد	rosoom al-bareed	postage
بريد لخارج الدولة	bareed le-khaarej ad-dawlah	postage abroad
الرمز البريدي	ar-ramz al-bareedee	post code
يحفظ بمكتب البريد	yoHfaz be-maktab al-bareed	poste restante
مكتب البريد	maktab al-bareed	post office
خطاب مسجل	kheTaab mosajal	registered mail
الراسل	ar-raasel	sender
طابع بريد	Taabeʌ bareed	stamp
طوابع	Tawaabeʌ	stamps

COMMUNICATIONS

Telephones: The telephone service varies greatly depending where you are in the Arab world. In the bigger towns and cities the telephone service rivals anything to be found in Europe or North America, with direct dialling to many countries as well as extensive mobile phone networks and efficient fax and on-line links. In more remote areas you may still need to go to a large central post office or an international hotel, where there will be a special section with an English-speaking operator. Most cafés will have a telephone suitable for making local calls. In an emergency even the most remote police station or hospital will have a telephone or radio-telephone they may let you use. In many parts of the Arab world public telephones in the street are unheard of and you will need to have a coffee in a café or a hotel as a way of getting access to a telephone – although things are beginning to change and public call-boxes are being installed in some areas.

USEFUL WORDS AND PHRASES

answering machine	ansur-foon
call	mokaalamah
to call	yatasel
crossed line	khoTooT telefoon moshtabekah
to dial	yodeer qors at-telefoonee
dialling tone	Sawt elteqaat al-khaT at-telefoon
extension	telefoon faraee
internet	intarnet
mobile phone	jawwaal, maHmool
modem	moodim
number	raqam
operator	sentraal
payphone	telefoon Aomoomi

phonecard	kaart telefoon
photocopier	makanit taoweer ol mostanadaat
receiver	samaAah
telephone box	koshk telefoon
telephone directory	daleel at-telefoon
Web site	mawqA Alal intarnet
wrong number	nomrah ghalaT

Where is the nearest phone box?
wayn aqrab koshk telefoon?

Can I use your telephone?
momken astaAmel teleefoonak?

Do you have change for the telephone?
Andak feraaTah meshaan at-teleefoon?

Can I call abroad from here?
momken atasel bel-khaarej men hona?

How much is a call to …?
be-kam al-mokaalamah le …?

How do I get an outside line?
kayf Ajeeb khat kharajee?

I would like to reverse the charges
oreed an yataHammal ash-shakhs al-maTloob moHaadathat-ho
thaman al-mokaalamah

I would like a number in …
oreed raqam fee …

Hello, this is … speaking
alloo, … yatakalam

Is that …?
hal haza …?

Speaking
yatakalam

I would like to speak to …
oreed atakalam maA …

Extension … please
farAee raqam … law samaнt

Please tell him … called
law samaнt qool laho … etasal

Ask him to call me back, please
law samaнt qool laho yaтlobnee

My number is …
raqamee …

Do you know where he is?
hal taAref howa wayn?

When will he be back?
emta be-yarjaA?

Could you leave him a message?
momken tatrok laho resaalah?

I'll ring back later
be-atasel behe marah thaaneeyah baAdayn

What's your fax number/email address?
ma raqam faaksak/ Aonwaanak fil ee-mail?

Did you get my fax/email?
hal Tasalamtu faaksee/ee-mailee?

Please resend your fax
law samaHt ta'bAth faaksak marrah thaneeyah

Can I send an email/fax from here?
momken abAth ee-mail/faaks min hona?

Can I use the photocopier/fax machine?
momken estakhdem makanit at-tasweer/faaks?

THINGS YOU'LL SEE

رمز	ramz	code
خط مباشر	khaTT mubaasher	direct dialling
طوارئ	Tawaare'	emergency
استعلامات	esteAlaamaat	enquiries
تصليح أعطال التليفونات	tasleeH AATaal at-telefoonaat	faults service
مكالمة دولية	mokaalamah duwaleeyah	international call
رسوم دولية	rosoom duwaleeyah	international charges
مكالمة محلية	mokaalamah maHaleeyah	local call
مكالمة مسافة بعيدة	mokaalamah masaafah baAeedah	long-distance call

→

موظف السنترال	**muwazzef as-sentraal**	operator
عاطل عن العمل	**ΑΑτel ΑΝ al-Αmal**	out of order
هاتف، تليفون	**haatef, telefoon**	telephone
كشك تليفون	**koshk telefoon**	telephone box

REPLIES YOU MAY BE GIVEN

toHeb tokallem meen?
Who would you like to speak to?

an-nomrah ghalaτ
You've got the wrong number

man yatakallam?
Who's speaking?

aysh nomratak?
What is your number?

aasef, howa maa mawjood
Sorry, he's not in

be-yarjaΑ as-saΑh …
He'll be back at … o'clock

law samaHt etasel marah thaaneeyah bokrah
Please call again tomorrow

sa-aqool laho enak etasalt
I'll tell him you called

SPORT

Sport in the Arab world does not suffer from the problem of rain and cold which commonly plagues many sporting pursuits in Northern Europe. In fact, the opposite is the case; it is often too hot to run around much anywhere near the middle of the day. It is only in very recent times that many Arab countries have given priority to the development of sporting facilities, although Egypt has a long tradition of football, golf and horse-racing.

Football is by far the most popular sport and the fortunes of major Western teams are avidly followed. Much of the huge length of coastline suitable for bathing and recreation remains undeveloped in most Arab countries, and for divers the Red Sea and Arabian Gulf boast some of the most spectacular coral reefs in the world. Gambling is frowned upon by Islam, but as a Westerner you will probably find a table somewhere in a 5-star hotel in Cairo, Alexandria, Amman or Damascus – but not in the cities of the Arabian peninsula. Backgammon, dominoes and chess are favourites in most Arab coffee shops.

Camel-racing and falconry are widely practised in Saudi Arabia and the other peninsular states. Both sports are keenly followed and visitors are well advised to enquire whether any events are scheduled in their region during their visit.

In common with other areas of Arab life, the participation of women in sporting activities is limited and women should have modest expectations of what will be open to them.

Useful Words and Phrases

athletics	al-alAab ar-riyaaDeeyah
badminton	badmentoon
ball	korrah
beach	shaaTe'
camel-racing	sebaaq al-jamal
canoe	kanoo
deck chair	korsee le-shaaTe' al-baHr
diving board	manasat ghaTs

falconry	sayd bes-soqoor
fishing	sayd as-samak
flippers	zeдanef
football	korrat qadam
golf	golf
golf course	malдb golf
gymnastics	jombaaz
harpoon	romн khaas les-sayd
hockey	hookee
horse-racing	sebaaq al-khayl
jogging	al-jaree al-khafeef
mountaineering	tasalloq al-jebaal
oxygen bottles	anaabeeb oksoojeen
pedal boat	markeb yoнmal bed-dawaaraat
racket	maдreb
riding	rokoob al-kayl
rowing boat	markeb tajdeef
to run	yajree
sailboard	lawн shoraдee
sailing	ebнaar
sea	baнr
skin diving	sebaaнah тант al-maa' be-esteдmaal jehaaz let-tanaffos
snorkel	shnorkel
stadium	estaad
to swim	yasbaн
swimming pool	нamaam sebaaнah
tennis	tennes
tennis court	malдb tennes
tennis racket	maдreb tennes
underwater fishing	sayd as-samak bel-ghaws тант al-maa'
volleyball	korrat таa'erah
walking	mashee
water-skiing	al-enzelaaq дla soтн al-maa'
water-skis	zalaaqat miyaah
wet suit	badlah lel-ghaws тант al-maa'
yacht	yakht

How do I get to the beach?
wayn aт-тareeq le-shaaтe' al-baнr?

How deep is the water here?
qad aysh ʌomq al-maay hona?

Is there an indoor/outdoor pool here?
hal fee нamaam sebaaнah daakhelee/khaarejee hona?

Is it safe to swim here?
hal as-sebaaнah hona amaan?

Can I fish here?
momken asтaad samak hona?

Do I need a licence?
hal oreed rokhsah?

I'd like to hire a sunshade
oreed asta'jer shamseeyah

How much does it cost per hour/day?
kam tatakallef kol saʌh/yawm?

I would like to take water-skiing lessons
oreed aakhoz doroos taʌllom al-enzelaaq ʌla soтн al-maa'

Where can I hire ...?
men wayn aqdar asta'jer ...?

I want to hire a sailboard
oreed asta'jer lawн shoraʌee

We'd like to see some camel-racing
noreed noshaahed sebaaq al-jamal

THINGS YOU'LL SEE

شاطئ البحر	shaaTe' al-baHr	beach
دراجات	darraajaat	bicycles
ملعب كرة قدم	malAb korrat qadam	football pitch
للإيجار	lel-eejaar	for hire
شرطة الميناء	shorTat al-meenaa	harbour police
ممنوع الغطس	mamnooA al-ghaTs	no diving
ممنوع الاستحمام	mamnooA al-esteHmaam	no swimming
ميناء	meenaa'	port
ميدان سباق	meedaan sebaaq	racecourse
منطقة مقيدة	manTaqah moqayadah	restricted area
مراكب شراعية	maraakeb shoraAeeyah	sailing boats
مركز الرياضة	markaz ar-rayaaDah	sports centre
إستاد	estaad	stadium
ملعب تنس	malAb tennes	tennis court
تذاكر	tazaaker	tickets

HEALTH

Wherever you travel in the Arab world you should ensure that you are properly insured for all health risks: accident, illness and any subsequent hospitalization. The Arab world covers an immense geographical area and includes regions where malaria is endemic – not to mention many other unusual and unpleasant illnesses which are rare or not found in Europe or North America. Before you leave you should consult your doctor about any particular immunisations that are needed for the area you are travelling to.

If you only drink bottled beverages, including water, you will avoid many potential gastric hazards. Similarly you should wash fruit and vegetables thoroughly or, preferably, peel them.

The general standard of medical care varies greatly from country to country; from the most modern and sophisticated facilities in a large city like Riyadh to fairly rudimentary arrangements in many rural parts. Take a good supply of any special medication you need as it may be difficult or impossible to obtain it where you are staying. If you do need to purchase drugs or medicines you should look for a pharmacy (**farmaasheeyah**). A prescription is usually unnecessary for drugs which are not dangerous and which can be bought over the counter.

If you need a doctor, you'll find that they tend to be grouped together in large practices, or clinics – Ay**aadah**. Within these clinics there will be a range of specialist doctors as well as some general practitioners. You will be expected to pay cash and it will be up to you to reclaim the expense from your insurance company later.

In general terms, the Arab world is conducive to good health, being very sunny, warm and dry. It should not be forgotten that the sun in sub-tropical latitudes can be extremely dangerous, particularly to fair-skinned Europeans and North Americans, and the greatest caution should be exercised when sunbathing or working out of doors. Not for nothing do the Bedouin desert-dwellers cover themselves almost completely when they go about in the sun.

USEFUL WORDS AND PHRASES

accident	Haadeth
ambulance	Arabat esAaf
anaemic	faqr ad-dam
appendicitis	eltehaab az-zaa'edah ad-doodeeyah
appendix	az-zaa'edah ad-doodeeyah
aspirin	'aspirin'
asthma	raboo
backache	alam feez-zahr
bandage	rebaaTah
bite (by dog)	ADDah
(by insect)	ladghah
bladder	mathaanah
blister	faqfooqah
blood	damm
blood donor	motabarreA bed-damm
burn	Harq
cancer	saraTaan
chemist	saydaleeyah
chest	sadr
chickenpox	jodayree
cholera	koolera
cold	zokaam
concussion	ertejaaj
constipation	emsaak
contact lenses	Adasaat laaseqah
corn	kaaloo
cough	soAal
cut	jarH
dentist	Tabeeb asnaan
diabetes	mosaab be-maraD as-sokkar
diarrhoea	es-haal
dizzy	daa'ekh
doctor	Tabeeb
(form of address)	doktoor
earache	wajaA al-ozon

fever	Homma
first aid	esAafaat awaleeyah
flu	enflooenza
fracture	kasr
gastroenteritis	eltehaab al-meAdah
German measles	al-Hasbah al-almaaneeyah
haemorrhage	nazeef damawee
hay fever	Homa al-qash
headache	sodaA
heart	qalb
heart attack	nawbah qalbeeyah
hospital	mostashfa
ill	mareeD
indigestion	Aosr haDm
inhaler (for asthma etc)	bakh-khaa-khah
injection	Hoqnah
itch	Hakkah
kidney	kolwah
lump	tawarrom feel-jesm
malaria	malaarya
measles	maraD al-Hasbah
migraine	sodaA nesfee
mumps	eltehaab al-ghoddah an-nakfeeyah
nausea	ghathayaan an-nafs
nurse (female)	momarreDah
operation	Amaleeyah
optician	Tabeeb Aoyoon
pain	alam
penicillin	'penicillin'
plaster (sticky)	blaaster
plaster of Paris	jebs
pneumonia	eltehaab re'awee
pregnant	Haamel
prescription	rooshettah
rheumatism	roomaatezm
scald	samT al-jeld
scratch	Hakkah jeldeeyah

sore throat	eHteqaan az-zoor
splinter	shazeeyah
sprain	malkh
sting	ladagh
stomach	meAdah
temperature	Haraarah
tonsils	lewaz al-Halq
toothache	wajaA asnaan
travel sickness	erhaaq wa maraD as-safar
ulcer	qorHah
vaccination	taTAeem
to vomit	yataqaya'
whooping cough	as-soAal ad-deekee
yellow fever	Homaa safra'

I have a pain in …
Andee wajaA fee …

I do not feel well
ashAor be-taAb

I feel faint
ashAor be-eghmaa'

I feel sick
uoreed ataqa'

I feel dizzy
ashAor be-dawkhah

I want to go to the clinic
oreed arooH el al-Ayaadah

It hurts here
aHess be-wajaA hona

It's a sharp pain
enaho wajaA Haad

It's a dull pain
enaho wajaA maktoom

It hurts all the time
fee wajaA daa'em

It only hurts now and then
fee wajaA aHyaanan

It hurts when you touch it
aHess be-wajaA Andama almes-ha

It hurts more at night
aHess be-wajaA akthar athnaa' al-layl

It stings/It aches
wajaA laadegh/mo'lemah

I have a temperature
darajat Haraartee mortafeAah

I need a prescription for …
oreed rooshettah le …

I normally take …
Aadatan aakhoz …

I'm allergic to …
Andee Hasaaseeyah men …

Have you got anything for …?
hal Andak ay dawaa' le …?

Do I need a prescription for ...?
hal oreed rooshettah le ...?

I'm ... months pregnant
ana hamil munzo ... shohoor

Can you take these if you're pregnant/breastfeeding?
momkin akhoz-ha law haamil/baraDaa?

I have lost a filling
saqaT Hashwo aHad asnaanee

THINGS YOU'LL SEE

عربة إسعاف	Arabat esAaf	ambulance
ضغط الدم	DaghT ad-dam	blood pressure
كشف عام	kashf Aam	check-up
عيادة	Aayaadah	clinic
طبيب أسنان	Tabeeb asnaan	dentist
طبيب	Tabeeb	doctor
دكتور	doktoor	doctor (title)
الصيدلية المداومة	as-saydaleeyah al-modaawemah	duty chemist
طوارئ	Tawaare'	Emergencies
حشو	Hashwo	filling
مركز الإسعافات الأولية	markaz al-esAsfaat al-awaleeyah	First Aid Post
نظارات	nazaaraat	glasses

→

مستشفى	**mostashfaa**	hospital
حقنة	**Hoqnah**	injection
دواء	**dawaa'**	medicine
على معدة خالية	**Ala meaAdah khaaleeyah**	on an empty stomach
طبيب عيون	**Tabeeb Aoyoon**	optician
روشتة	**rooshettah**	prescription
عيادة طبيب	**Aayaadat Tabeeb**	surgery
أشعة	**asheAah**	X-ray

THINGS YOU'LL HEAR

khoz ... qors/Habah kol marah
Take ... pills/tablets at a time

maA al-miyaah
With water

emDagh-hom
Chew them

marah/maratayn/thalaath maraat yawmeeyan
Once/twice/three times a day

Andama tanaam faqaT
Only when you go to bed

Aadatan taakhoz ay nawA?
What do you normally take?

laazem yakoon maAk rooshettah le-haza ad-dawaa'
For that you need a prescription

MINI-DICTIONARY

about: about 16 Hawaalee 16
accelerator dawaasat al-banzeen
accident Haadethah
accommodation maskan
ache wajaA
adaptor (electrical) waseelah mohaaye'ah
address Aonwaan
adhesive (noun) maadah laaseqah
admission charge rasm ad-dokhool
after baAd
aftershave kolooniya ler-rejaal
again marah okhrah
against Ded
air conditioning mokayyef
aircraft Taa'grah
air freshener moATTer
air hostess moDeefah jaweeyah
airline khaT Tayaraan
airport maTaar
alarm clock monabbeh
alcohol koHool
Algeria al-jazaa'er
all kol, jameeA
    all the streets jameeA ash-shawaareA
    that's all, thanks khalaas, shokran
almost taqreeban
already alaan
always daa'eman
am: I am ana
ambulance esAaf
America amreeka
American (man) amreekaanee
    (woman) amreekaaneeyah
    (adj) amreekaanee
Ancient Egypt masr al-qadeemah
Ancient Egyptians al-qodamaa'
    al-masreeyeen
and wa
ankle kaatel
104

anorak baalToo qaseer
another (different) aakhar
    (additional) eDaafee
answering machine al-ansur-foon
antifreeze moDaad let-tajmeed
antique shop matjar al-Aadeeyaat
antiseptic moTahher
apartment shaqqah
aperitif mosh-hee
appetite shaheeyah
apple tofaaH
application form estemaarah
appointment meeAad
apricot meshmesh
are: you are (masculine) anta
    (feminine) anti
    we are eHna
    they are hom
arm zeraA
art fann
art gallery matHaf fonoon
artist fanaan
as: as soon as possible be-asraA ma
    yomken
ashtray menfaDat sejaa'er
asleep: he's asleep howa naa'em
aspirin aspereen
at: at the post office fee maktab al-bareed
    at night feel-layl
    at 3 o'clock as-saAh 3 (thalaath)
attractive jameel
aunt (maternal) khaalah
    (paternal) Ammah
Australia ostraaliya
Australian (man) ostraalee
    (woman) ostraaleeyah
    (adj) ostraalee
Austria an-nemsa
automatic otoomaateek

away: is it far away? hal howa baAeed jeddan?
 go away! emshee!
awful haa'el
axe fa'as
axle meHwar al-Ajalah

baby Tefl raDeeA
baby wipes waraa'il atfaal
back (not front) khalf
 (body) zohr
bad radee'
Bahrain al-baHrayn
bake yakhbez
baker khabaaz
balcony balkoonah
ball korrah
ball point pen qalam jaaf
banana mooz
band (musicians) ferqah
bandage rabaaTah
bank bank
banknote waraqah naqdeeyah
bar bar
 bar of chocolate
 qeTaat shokoolaatah
barbecue mashwee Alal-faHm
barber's Halaaq
bargain safqah
basement badroom
basin (sink) HawD
basket sallah
bath baanyo
 to have a bath yastaHemm
bathroom Hamaam
battery baTaareeyah
bazaar souq
beach shaaTee'
beans fool
beard leHyah
because Alashaan
bed sareer
bed linen melaayaat as-sareer

bedroom ghorfat an-nawm
beef laHm baqar
beer beerah
before qabl
beginner mobtadee'
behind khalf
beige bayj
Belgium beljeeka
bell jaras
belly dance raqs baladee
below asfal
belt Hezaam
beside be-jaaneb
best afDal
better aHsan
between ma bayn
bicycle daraajah
big kabeer
bikini bekeenee
bill faatoorah
bin liner beTaanat sandooq al-qomaamah
bird Asfoor
birthday ayd meelaad
 happy birthday! Ayd meelaad saAeed!
birthday present hadeeyat Ayd al-meelaad
biscuit baskooweet
bite (verb) ADD
 (noun) ADDah
 (by insect) ladghah
bitter morr
black aswad
blackberry Awsaj shaa'eA
blanket baTaaneeyah
blind (cannot see) aAma
blinds setaarah
blister faqfooqah
blood damm
blouse bloozah
blue azraq
boat markab
 (smaller) qaareb
body jesm

boil (verb) ya<u>gh</u>lee

bolt (verb) tarb<u>a</u>sa
(noun: on door) terb<u>aa</u>s

bone azm

bonnet (car) boon<u>ee</u>t

book (noun) ket<u>aa</u>b
(verb) ya<u>H</u>jez

booking office m<u>a</u>ktab al-<u>H</u>ajz

bookshop makt<u>a</u>bah

boot (car) <u>shanTat as-sayaa</u>rah
(footwear) <u>H</u>ez<u>aa</u>'

border Hod<u>oo</u>d

boring mom<u>e</u>ll

born: I was born in
<u>a</u>na mawl<u>oo</u>d fee …

both kol<u>aa</u>

both of them kol<u>ee</u>yat-h<u>o</u>ma
both of us <u>e</u>Hna al-ethn<u>a</u>yn
both … and … … wa …

bottle zoj<u>aa</u>jah

bottle opener fat<u>aaH</u>at zoj<u>aaj</u>aat

bottom (of sea, box etc) q<u>a</u>A

bowl we<u>A</u>a'

box s<u>a</u>ndooq

boy w<u>a</u>lad

bra sootiy<u>aa</u>n

bracelet sew<u>aa</u>r

braces Hamaal<u>aa</u>t al-banTal<u>oo</u>n

brake (noun) m<u>e</u>kbaH
(verb) y<u>a</u>kbaH

brandy br<u>aa</u>ndee

bread khobz

breakdown (car) ta<u>A</u>Tal
(nervous) enhiy<u>aa</u>r

breakfast eft<u>aa</u>r

breathe yatan<u>a</u>ffas
I can't breathe ma <u>a</u>qdar atan<u>a</u>ffas

bridge k<u>oo</u>bree

briefcase <u>shan</u>Tah

British breeT<u>aa</u>nee

brochure br<u>oo</u>cher

broken maks<u>oo</u>r
broken leg rejl maks<u>oo</u>rah

brooch broosh

brother akh

brown b<u>o</u>nnee

bruise k<u>a</u>dmah

brush (noun) mekn<u>a</u>sah
(paint) f<u>o</u>rshaah
(verb) y<u>a</u>knos

bucket j<u>a</u>rdal

building ben<u>aa</u>yah

bumper madAm<u>ee</u>yah

burglar less

burn (verb) y<u>aH</u>req
(noun) Harq

bus baas

bus station ma<u>H</u>aTTat baas<u>aa</u>t

business <u>sh</u>oghl
it's none of your business!
mesh <u>sh</u>oghlak!

busy (occupied) mash<u>gh</u>ool
(bar) mozda<u>H</u>em

but l<u>a</u>ken

butcher jaz<u>aa</u>r

butter z<u>e</u>bdah

button zor<u>aa</u>r

buy ya<u>sh</u>taree

by: by the window be-j<u>aa</u>neb
a<u>sh</u>-<u>sh</u>ob<u>aa</u>k
by Friday be-H<u>o</u>l<u>oo</u>l yawm al-j<u>o</u>m<u>A</u>h
by myself be-wa<u>H</u>dee

cabbage k<u>o</u>ronb

cable TV k<u>aa</u>bil

café m<u>a</u>qhaa

cake kayk

calculator <u>aa</u>lat H<u>aa</u>sebah

call: what's it called?
shoo esm<u>a</u>ha?

camel j<u>a</u>mal

camera k<u>aa</u>mera

campsite mo<u>A</u>skar

camshaft Am<u>oo</u>d al-k<u>aa</u>mah

can (tin) <u>A</u>olbah

can: can I have …? m<u>o</u>mken <u>aa</u>khoz …?

Canada k<u>a</u>nada

Canadian (man) kanadee
  (woman) kanadeeyah
  (adj) kanadee
cancer sarataan
candle shamAah
canoe kaanoo
cap (bottle) ghetaa'
  (hat) barneetah
car sayaarah
car seat (for a baby) korsee atfaal
caravan karafaan
carburettor karboraateer
card kaart
careful Hazer
  be careful! khoz baalak!
carpet sejaadah
carriage (train) Arabah
carrot jazar
case (affair) qadeeyah
  (container) kees
cash kaash, naqdan
  (coins) Aomlah
  to pay cash yadfaA kaash,
  yadfaA naqdan
cassette kaaseet
cassette player mosajjel
castle qasr
cat qettah
catacombs saraadeeb
cathedral kaatedraa'eeyah
cauliflower qarnabeet
cave kahf
cemetery maqbarah
centre markaz
certificate shahaadah
chair korsee
chambermaid khaademah fee fondoq
change (noun: money) fakkah
  (verb: clothes) yoghayyer
cheap rakhees
cheers! (health) fee seHatak!
cheese jebnah
chemist (shop) saydaleeyah
cheque sheek

chequebook daftar sheekaat
cherry kareez
chess shatranj
chessboard lawHat ash-shatranj
chest (anatomical) sadr
chewing gum masteekah
chicken dojaaj
child tefl
children atfaal
china fakhaar
China as-seen
Chinese (man) seenee
  (woman) seeneeyah
  (adj) seenee
chips sheebs
chocolate shokoolaatah
  box of chocolates Aolbat
  shokoolaatah
chop (food) delaHma
  (to cut) yaqtaA
Christian name esm
church kaneesah
cigar seejaar
cigarette seejaarah
cinema seenema
city madeenah
city centre wasat al-madeenah
class fasl
classical Arabic al-loghat
  al-Arabeeyah al-fos-Ha
classical music mooseeqa
  klaaseekeeyah
clean nazeef
clear (obvious) waadeH
  (water) naqee
  is that clear?
  hal haza waadeH
clever shaater
clock saAh
close (near) qareeb
  (stuffy) khaaneq
  (verb) yoghleq
  the shop is closed
  ad-dokaan moghlaq

clothes mal<u>aa</u>bes

club n<u>aa</u>dee

(cards) seb<u>aa</u>tee

clutch debriy<u>aa</u>j

coach baas

(of train) <u>A</u>rabat al-qeT<u>aa</u>r

coach station maH<u>a</u>TTat al-baas<u>aa</u>t

coat baalT<u>oo</u>

coat hanger shamg<u>A</u>h

cockroach sars<u>oo</u>r

coffee q<u>a</u>hwah

coffee pot k<u>a</u>nakah

coin <u>A</u>omlah

cold (illness) zok<u>aa</u>m

(adj) bard

(weather) b<u>aa</u>red

collar y<u>aa</u>qah

collection (stamps etc) majm<u>oo</u>Ah

colour lawn

colour film feelm mol<u>a</u>wwan

comb (noun) meshT

(verb) y<u>a</u>msheT

come y<u>a</u>'atee

I come from … <u>a</u>na men …

we came last week wasalna al-osb<u>oo</u>A al-m<u>aa</u>Dee

come here! t<u>A</u>a h<u>e</u>na!

compartment maqs<u>oo</u>rah

complicated mo<u>A</u>qad

concert H<u>a</u>flah mooseeq<u>ee</u>yah

conditioner (hair) mon<u>A</u>em lesh-sh<u>A</u>r

conductor (bus) moH<u>a</u>ssel taz<u>aa</u>ker

(orchestra) q<u>aa</u>'ed f<u>e</u>rqah mooseeq<u>ee</u>yah

congratulations! mabr<u>oo</u>k!

constipation ems<u>aa</u>k

consulate qonsol<u>ee</u>yah

contact lenses <u>A</u>das<u>aa</u>t laas<u>e</u>qah

contraceptive m<u>aa</u>neA lel-H<u>a</u>ml

cook (noun) Tab<u>aa</u>kh

(verb) y<u>a</u>Tbokh

cooking utensils aw<u>aa</u>nee aT-T<u>a</u>haa

cool b<u>aa</u>red

108

copper naH<u>aa</u>s

cork fel<u>ee</u>z

corkscrew bar<u>ee</u>mah

corner rokn

corridor mam<u>a</u>rr

cosmetics mostaHD<u>a</u>r<u>aa</u>t let-tajm<u>ee</u>l

cost (verb) yok<u>a</u>llef

what does it cost? aysh at-takl<u>e</u>fah

cotton qoTn

cotton wool qoTn T<u>e</u>bbee

cough (verb) y<u>a</u>sAl

(noun) so<u>A</u>al

country (state) d<u>a</u>wlah

(not town) ary<u>aa</u>f

cousin (male) (paternal) ebn <u>A</u>mm

(maternal) ebn khaal

(female) (paternal) bent <u>A</u>mm

(maternal) bent khaal

crab saraT<u>aa</u>n al-b<u>a</u>Hr

cramp taq<u>a</u>ll<u>o</u>s al-<u>A</u>D<u>a</u>laat

crayfish salT<u>aA</u>oon

cream kreem

credit card beT<u>aa</u>qat e<u>A</u>tem<u>aa</u>d

crew T<u>aa</u>qem

crisps baT<u>aa</u>Tes sheeps

crowded mozd<u>a</u>Hem

cruise j<u>a</u>wlah baHr<u>ee</u>yah

crutches <u>A</u>ok<u>aa</u>z

cry (weep) y<u>a</u>bkee

(shout) yas<u>ee</u>H

cucumber khiy<u>aa</u>r

cuff links zerr kom al-qam<u>ee</u>s

cup fenj<u>aa</u>n

cupboard dool<u>aa</u>b

curls taj<u>A</u>eed wa tamw<u>ee</u>j ash-sh<u>a</u>Ar

curry k<u>aa</u>ree

curtain set<u>aa</u>rah

customs j<u>o</u>mrok

cut (noun) qaTA

(verb) y<u>a</u>qTaA

dad b<u>a</u>ba

dairy (shop) dok<u>aa</u>n b<u>a</u>ysA al-alb<u>aa</u>n

damp raTb

dance raqs

dangerous khaTar

dark moz_a_llem

daughter _e_bnah

day yawm

dead mayt

deaf _a_Trash

dear (person) _a_z_ee_z

(expensive) ghaalee

deck chair kors_ee_ le-shaaTe' al-b_a_Hr

deep _a_m_ee_q

deliberately _a_mdan

dentist Tab_ee_b asn_aa_n

dentures Taqam asn_aa_n

deny yonker

deodorant moz_ee_l raa'_e_Hat al-_a_rq

department store dok_aa_n kab_ee_r

zo aqs_aa_m motan_a_ww_e_Ah

departure raH_ee_l

desert saH_a_raa'

develop (film) yoH_a_mmeD

diamond (jewel) al-m_aa_s

(cards) ad-deen_aa_ree

diarrhoea es-h_aa_l

diary mof_a_kkerah

dictionary qaam_oo_s

die yam_oo_t

diesel d_ee_zel

different mokht_a_lef

that's different

haz_aa_k mokht_a_lef

I'd like a different one

or_ee_d n_a_wA mokht_a_lef

difficult s_a_Ab

dining car _a_rabat al-'akl

dining room gh_o_rfat aT-T_a_Am

directory (telephone) dal_ee_l

dirty q_a_zer

disabled _a_ajez

disposable nappies Hafaad_aa_t

distributor (car) destr_e_byooter

dive yaghT_a_s

diving board m_a_nsat al-ghaTes

divorced (man) moT_a_llaq

(woman) moT_a_llaqah

do y_a_amal

doctor Tab_ee_b

document wath_ee_qah

dog kalb

doll _a_roosah

dollar dollar

door baab

double room gh_o_rfah be-sar_ee_r

mozd_a_wej

doughnut fat_ee_rah

down _a_sfal

drawing pin dab_oo_s rasm

dress fost_aa_n

drink (verb) yashrab

(noun) mashr_oo_b

would you like a drink? tor_ee_d

t_a_shrab shay'?

drinking water maa' lesh-shorb

drive (verb) yas_oo_q

driver saa'eq

driving licence r_o_khsat qiy_aa_dah

drunk sakr_aa_n

dry jaaf

dry cleaner tanz_ee_f al-mal_aa_bes

bel-bokh_aa_r

dummy (for baby) H_a_lamah

maT_aa_T_ee_yah ler-raD_ee_A

during khel_aa_l

dustbin safeeHah al-qom_aa_mah

duster menf_a_Dah

duty-free mo_a_faa men ar-r_a_sm al-jomrokee

each (every) kol

twenty dinars each kol w_aa_Hed

be-_a_eshr_ee_n d_ee_nar

early mob_a_kker

earrings H_a_laqah

ears _o_zon

east sharq

easy s_a_hel

eat y_a_'kol

egg bayD
Egypt mesr
either: either of them ay menhoma
    either ... or ema ... aw ...
elastic maren
elastic band laasteek
elbow kooA
electric kahrabaa'ee
electricity kahrabaa'
else: something else shay' aakhar
    someone else shakhs aakhar
    somewhere else makaan aakhar
email ee-mail
email address Aonwaan il-eemail
embarrassing mokhbel
embassy sefaarah
embroidery taTreez
emerald zomorrod
emergency Tawaare'
Emirates al-emaaraat
empty khaalee
end nehaayah
engaged (couple) makhTooB
    (occupied) mashghool
engine (motor) moHarrek
England engeltera
English engleezee
    (language) engleezee
Englishman engleezee
Englishwoman engleezeeyah
enlargement takbeer
enough kefaayah
entertainment tasleeyah
entrance madkhal
envelope mazroof
escalator masAd
especially makhsoos
evening masaa'
every kol
everyone kol waaHed
everything kol shay'
everywhere kol makaan
example methaal
    for example Ala sabeel al-methaal
110

excellent momtaaz
excess baggage wazn zaa'ed
exchange (verb) yoHawwel
exchange rate seAr at-taHweel
excursion nozhah
excuse me! (to get attention) law samaHt!
exit makhraj
expensive ghaalee
extension tamdeed
eye drops qaTarah lel-Aynayn
eyes Aynayn

face wajh
faint (unclear) baahet
    (verb) yagheeb An al-waAee
    to feel faint yashAor be-eghmaa'
fair (funfair) malaahee
    (just) it's not fair laysa haza
    Aadel
false teeth asnaan senaAeeyah
family Aa'elah
fan (ventilator) marwaHah
    (enthusiast) moAjab
fan belt sayr al-marwaHah
far baAeed
    how far is ...? qad aysh
    al-masaafah le-...?
fare ojrat as-safar
farm mazraA
farmer mozaareA
fashion al-mooDah
fast sareA
    (noun: during Ramadan etc) soom
fat (of person) badeen
    (on meat etc) dehn
father ab
fax machine makanit faaks
feel (touch) yalmes
    I feel hot ashAor be-sokhoonah
    I feel like ... ashAor be ...
    I don't feel well seHatee laysat
    Ala ma yoraam
feet qadam

ferry moAdeeyah
fever Homma
fiancé khateeb
fiancée khateebah
field Haql
fig teen
filling *(tooth)* Hashoo
film feelm
filter felter
finger osboA
fire naar
　(blaze) Hareeq
fire extinguisher Tafaayat Hareeq
fireworks alAab naareeyah
first awal
　first aid esAafaat awaleeyah
　first floor aT-Taabeq al-awal
fish samak
fishing sayd as-samak
　to go fishing
　yazhab le-sayd as-samak
fishing rod qasabat sayd as-samak
fishmonger baa'eA as-samak
fizzy fawaar
flag Alam
flash *(camera)* flaash
flat *(level)* mosaTTaH
　(apartment) shaqqah
flavour TAAm
flea borghooth
flight reHlat Tayaraan
flip-flops shebsheb
flippers zAAnef
flour daqeeq
flower zahrah
flu enflooenza
fly *(verb)* yaTeer
　(insect) zobaabah
fog Dabaab
folk music mooseeqa shaAbeeyah
food TAAm
food poisoning tasammom ghezaa'ee
football korrat qadam
　(ball) korrah

for le
　for me lee
　what for? lemaaza?
　for a week le-modat osbooA
foreigner ajnabee
forest ghaabah
fork shawkah
fortnight osbooAyn
fountain pen qalam Hebr
fourth ar-raabeA
fracture kasr
France faransa
free khaalee
　(no cost) majaanan
freezer freezer
French faransee
fridge thalaajah
friend sadeeq
friendly lateef
front: in front of … amaam …
frost saqeeA
fruit faakeha
fruit juice Aseer fawaakeh
fry yaqlee
frying pan taasah lel-qalee
full momtale'
　I'm full ana shabAan
full board eqaamah bel-ma'kal
funnel *(for pouring)* qomA
funny moDHek
　(odd) ghareeb
furniture athaath

garage garaaj
garden Hadeeqah
garlic thoom
gear sondooq at-teroos
gear lever naaqel sondooq at-teroos
German almaanee
Germany alemaaniya
get *(fetch)* yajeeb
　have you got …? Andak …?
　to get the train yalHaq al-qetaar

get back: we get back tomorrow
  narjaA bokrah
    to get something back yorajjeA
get in yadkhol
    (arrive) yaSel
get out yakhroj
get up (rise) yaqoom
gift hadeeyah
gin jenn
girl bent
give yoATee
glad masroor
    I'm glad ana masroor
glass zojaaj
    (to drink) koob
glasses nazaraat
gloss prints Tebaah laameAh
gloves qafaazaat
glue samgh
goggles nazaraat khaasah le-weqaayat
    al-Aynayn
gold zahab
good jayyed
    good! wa howa ka-zaalek!
goodbye maA as-salaamah
government Hokoomah
granddaughter Hafeedah
grandfather jadd
grandmother jaddah
grandson Hafeed
grapes Aenab
grass Aoshb
Great Britain breeTaaniya al-AoZma
Greece al-yoonaan
Greek yoonaanee
green akhDar
grey ramaadee
grill shawaayah
grocer (shop) baqaal
ground floor aT-Taabeq al-arDee
guarantee (noun) Damaan
    (verb) yaDman
guard Haares
guide book daleel as-soyaaH
112

guitar geetaar
Gulf al-khaleej
Gulf States dowwal al-khaleej
gun (rifle) bondoqeeyah
    (pistol) mosaddas

hair shaAr
haircut (for man) Helaaqat ash-shaAr
    (for woman) qass ash-shaAr
hairdresser Halaaq
hair dryer mojaffef ash-shaAr
hair spray Telaa' yobakh
    Alash-shaAr le-tathbeet-ho
half nesf
    half an hour nesf saAh
half board nawm wa efTaar faqaT
hamburger hamborger
hammer meTraqah
hand yad
handbrake faraamel
handbag shanTat yad
handkerchief mandeel
handle (door) meqbaD
handsome waseem
hangover khomaar
happy saAeed
harbour meenaa'
hard qaasee
    (difficult) saAb
hard (contact) lenses Adasaat saldeeyah
hat qobaAh
have (own) yamtalek
    I don't have ... ma Andee ...
    can I have ...? momken aakhoz ...?
    have you got ...? Andak ...?
    I have to go now
    laazem amshee alaan
hay fever al-Homma al-qasheeyah
he howa
head ra's
headache sodaA
headlights an-noor al-amaamee
hear yasmaA

hearing aid samaAt al-asamm
heart qalb
heart attack nawbah qalbeeyah
heating tadfe'ah
heavy thaqeel
heel kaAb
hello ahlan
help (noun) mosaAdah
  (verb) yosaAed
  help! an-najdah!
hepatitis as-sufraa
her: it's her haza heya
  it's for her haza laha
  give it to her aATeeha laha
  (possessive) ...-ha
  her book ketaabha
  her house manzelha
  her shoes Hezaa'ha
  it's hers haza melk ha
here hona
hieroglyphs heerooghleefee
high Aalee
highway code
  taAleemaat al-qiyaadah
hill tell
him: it's him haza howa
  it's for him haza laho
  give it to him aATeeha laho
hire yasta'jer
his ...-ho
  his book ketaabho
  his house manzelho
  his shoes Hezaa'ho
  it's his haza melk-ho
history taareekh
hitchhiking otostop
HIV positive mareeD HIV
hobby hawaayah
Holland holanda
holiday AoTlah
homeopathy Ajlaaj mithlee
honest saadeq
honey Asal
honeymoon shahr al-Asal

horn (car) booq
  (animal) qarn
horrible mofzeA
hospital mostashfa
hot (weather) Haar
hour saAh
house manzel
how? kayf?
hungry: I'm hungry ana jawAan
hurry: I'm in a hurry
  ana mostaAjel
husband zawj

I ana
ice thalj
ice cream ays kreem
ice cube qeTAt thalj
ice lolly masaasah
if eza
ignition jehaaz al-eshAal
ill mareeD
immediately fawran
impossible mostaHeel
in fee
  in English bel-engleezee
  in the hotel feel-fondoq
India al-hend
Indian (man) hendee
  (woman) hendeeyah
  (adj) hendee
indicator mo'asher
indigestion Aosr al-haDm
infection Adwa
information maAloomaat
inhaler (for asthma etc) bakh-khaa-khah
injection Hoqnah
injury jarH
ink Hebr
inner tube anboob daakhelee
insect Hasharah
insect repellent
  Taared lel-Hasharaat
insomnia araq

insurance ta'meen
interesting shayeq
internet intarnet
interpret yotarjem
invitation daawa
Iraq al-Aeraaq
Ireland erlanda
Irish erlandee
Irishman erlandee
Irishwoman erlandeeyah
iron (metal) Hadeed
  (for clothes) mekwah
ironmonger Hadaad
is: he is ... howa ...
  she is ... heya ...
Islam eslaam
island jazeerah
it howa, heya
  it's over there howa/hiya honaak
Italy eetaalya
itch (noun) Hakkah jeldeeyah
  it itches yoHekk

jacket jaakeet
jam morabba
jazz mooseeqa al-jazz
jealous ghayoor
jeans jeenz
jellyfish qandeel al-baHr
jeweller taajer mojawharaat
job wazeefah
jog (verb) hazz
  to go for a jog yajree be-hodoo'
  let-tarayoD
joke noktah
Jordan al-ordon
journey reHlah
jumper bloozah men at-treeko
just: it's just arrived qad wasalat haza
  al-laHzah
  I've just one left Andee waaHedah
  baaqeeyah faqaT
  just two ethnayn faqaT
114

key meftaaH
kidney kolyah
kilo keelo
kilometre keelometer
kitchen maTbakh
knee rokbah
knife sakeen
knit yaHook be-'ebr at-treeko
know: I don't know laa aAref
Koran qoraan
Kuwait al-koowayt

label beTaaqah
lace dantelah
laces (of shoe) rebaaT al-Heza'
lake boHayrah
lamb kharoof
lamp mesbaaH
lampshade abajoor
land (noun) arD
  (verb) yahboT
language loghah
large kabeer
last (final) akheer
  last week al-osbooA al-maaDee
  last month ash-shahr al-maaDee
  at last! akheeran!
late: it's getting late al-waqt mota'akher
  the bus is late al-bas mota'akher
laugh yaDHak
launderette dokaan le-ghasl ath-thiyaab
laundry (place) maghsal
  (dirty clothes) malaabes toreed al-ghasl
laxative mos-hel
lazy kaslaan
leaf waraqah
leaflet warayqah
learn yataAllam
leather jeld
Lebanon lebnaan
left (not right) yasaar
  there's nothing left la yoojad
  shay' motabaqee

left luggage *(locker)* khezaanah
lesh-shonoT

leg rejl

lemon laymoon

lemonade leemoonaadah

length Tool

lens Adasah

less aqall

lesson dars

letter kheTaab

letter box sandooq al-bareed

lettuce khass

library maktabah

Libya leebya

licence roksah

life Hayaah

lift *(in building)* mesAd
could you give me a lift?
momken towaselnee?

light *(not heavy)* khafeef
(not dark) faateH

light meter Adaad aD-Daw'

lighter qadaaHah

lighter fuel ghaaz al-qadaaHah

like: I like you ana moAjab bek
I like swimming ana oHebb
as-sebaaHah
it's like … enaho yoshbeh …

lime *(fruit)* laymoon maaleH

lip salve marham le-manaA tashaffof
ash-shafaah

lipstick qalam rooj

liqueur sharaab koHoolee Helw
al-mazaaq

list qaa'emah

litre leeter

litter qomaamah motanaatherah

little *(small)* sagheer
it's a little big enaha kabeerah
baAD ash-shay'
just a little kameeyah qaleelah faqaT

liver kabed

lobster jambaree kabeer al-Hajm

lollipop masaasah

long Taweel
how long does it take? qad aysh
tastaghreq?

lorry looree

lost property Haqaa'eb mafqoodah

lot: a lot kameeyah kabeerah

loud *(noise)* (sawt) Aalee
(colour) sarekh

lounge salat al-joloos

love *(noun)* Hobb
(verb) yoHebb

lover *(man)* Asheeq
(woman) Asheeqah

low monkhafeD

luck Hazz
good luck! Hazz saaeed!

luggage Haqaa'eb

luggage rack raff al-Haqaa'eb

lunch ghadaa'

magazine majallah

mail bareed

make yosawee

make-up makiyaaj

man rajol

manager modeer

map khareeTah
a map of Riyadh khareeTat
ar-riyaaD

marble zokhaam

margarine marjareen

market souq

marmalade morabba al-borto'aan

married motazawaj

mascara mekHal

mass *(church)* qodaas

mast saaren

match *(light)* Aood kebreet
(sport) mobaarah

material *(cloth)* qomaash

mattress martabah

Mauritania moretaaniya

maybe momken

me: it's me (speaking) ana atakallam
  it's for me enaho lee
  give it to me aaTeeneeho
meal wajbah
meat laHm
mechanic meekaaneekee
medicine dawaa'
meeting ejtemaA
melon shamaam
men's toilet towaaleet ler-rejaal
menu qaa'emat al-aTAemah
message resaalah
midday az-zohr
middle: in the middle feel-wasaT
midnight nesf al-layl
milk Haleeb
mine: it's mine haza melkee
mineral water miyaah maAdaneeyah
minute daqeeqah
mirror meraah
Miss aaneesah
mistake ghalTah
  to make a mistake yaghlaT
mobile phone jawwaal, maHmool
modem modim
monastery dayr
money foloos
month shahr
monument nosob tazkaaree
moon qamar
moped motoseeklett
more akthar
morning sabaaH
  in the morning fees-sabaaH
Morocco al-maghreb
mosaic fosayfesaa'
mosque jaameA
mosquito baAooDah
mother omm
motorbike daraajah bokhaareeyah
motorboat qaareb bokhaaree
motorway Tareeq ra'eesee
mountain jebel
mouse fa'r
116

moustache shaareb
mouth fam
move yataHarrak
  don't move! laa tataHarrak
  (house) yoAzzel
movies as-seenema
  a movie feelm seenemaa'ee
Mr as-sayed
Mrs as-sayedah
much: not much laysa katheer
  much better/slower
  afDal be-katheer/baTee' jeddan
muezzin mo'azzen
mug fenjaan
  a mug of coffee fenjaan qahwah
mule baghl
mum mama/om
museum matHaf
mushroom foTr
music mooseeqa
musical instrument adaah
  mooseeqeeyah
musician mooseeqaar
Muslim moslem
mussels omm al-kholool
mustard khardal
my ...-ee
  my book ketaabee
  my bag shanTatee
  my keys mafaateeHee
mythology asaaTeer al-qodamaa'

nail (metal) mesmaar
  (finger) azaafer
nailfile mebrad azaafer
nail polish molamme' lel-azaafer
name esm
nappy kafoolat aT-Tefl
narrow Dayeq
near: near the door qareeb men al-baab
  near London qareeb men London
necessary Darooree
necklace Aoqd

need (*verb*) yaнt<u>aa</u>j
  I need … aнt<u>aa</u>j …
  there's no need laa d<u>a</u>нee
needle '<u>e</u>brah
negative (*photo*) s<u>oo</u>rah
  fotoografee<u>ya</u>h salb<u>ee</u>yah
neither: neither of them laa
  w<u>aa</u>нed men h<u>o</u>ma
  neither … nor … laa … wa-l<u>aa</u> …
nephew (*brother's son*) ebn al-<u>a</u>kh
  (*sister's son*) ebn al-<u>o</u>kht
never <u>a</u>badan
new jad<u>ee</u>d
news akhb<u>aa</u>r
newsagent b<u>aa</u>'ea as-s<u>o</u>нof
newspaper jar<u>ee</u>dah
New Zealand niy<u>oo</u> zel<u>a</u>nda
New Zealander (*man*) niy<u>oo</u> zel<u>a</u>ndee
  (*woman*) niy<u>oo</u> zeland<u>ee</u>yah
next al-q<u>aa</u>dem
  next week al-'osb<u>oo</u>a al-q<u>aa</u>dem
  next month ash-sh<u>a</u>hr al-q<u>aa</u>dem
nice jam<u>ee</u>l
niece (*brother's daughter*) bent al-<u>a</u>kh
  (*sister's daughter*) bent al-<u>o</u>kht
night layl
nightclub n<u>aa</u>dee l<u>a</u>ylee
nightdress thowb an-n<u>a</u>wm len-nes<u>aa</u>'
night porter khaf<u>ee</u>r l<u>a</u>ylee
Nile an-n<u>ee</u>l
no (*response*) laa
  I have no money maa <u>A</u>ndee fol<u>oo</u>s
  there are no … maa fee …
noisy kath<u>ee</u>r aD-D<u>oo</u>Daa'
north shem<u>aa</u>l
Northern Ireland erl<u>a</u>nda
  ash-shemaal<u>ee</u>yah
nose anf
not laa, moo
notebook d<u>a</u>ftar molaakhaz<u>aa</u>t
nothing laa shay'
novel rew<u>aa</u>yah
now al<u>aa</u>n
number raqm

number plate l<u>a</u>wнat al-arq<u>aa</u>m
nurse (*female*) momarreD<u>a</u>h
nut (*fruit*) b<u>o</u>ndoq
  (*for bolt*) saam<u>oo</u>lah

obelisk mas<u>a</u>llah
occasionally aнy<u>aa</u>nan
octopus okht<u>o</u>b<u>oo</u>T
of men
office m<u>a</u>ktab
often gh<u>aa</u>leban
oil (*for food*) zayt
  (*car*) naft
oil industry sen<u>aa</u>t al-betr<u>oo</u>l
oil well be'r betr<u>oo</u>l
ointment m<u>a</u>rham
OK ook<u>a</u>y
old (*thing*) qad<u>ee</u>m
  (*person*) Aj<u>oo</u>z
olive zayt<u>oo</u>n
Oman Aom<u>aa</u>n
omelette ooml<u>ee</u>t
on <u>A</u>la
  on the ground <u>A</u>la al-<u>a</u>rD
  on the table <u>A</u>la aT-T<u>aa</u>walah
one w<u>aa</u>нed
onion b<u>a</u>sal
only f<u>a</u>qaT
open (*verb*) y<u>a</u>ftaн
  (*adj*) maft<u>oo</u>н
opposite: opposite the hotel
  am<u>aa</u>m al-f<u>o</u>ndoq
optician nazaar<u>aa</u>tee
or aw
orange (*colour*) bortoq<u>aa</u>lee
  (*fruit*) bortoq<u>aa</u>l
orange juice as<u>ee</u>r bortoq<u>aa</u>l
orchestra al-<u>oo</u>rkestra
ordinary (*normal*) <u>A</u>adee
organ A<u>o</u>Dw
  (*music*) al-<u>o</u>rghon
our …-na
  it's ours h<u>a</u>za m<u>e</u>lkna

out: he's out howa moo mawjood
outside khaarej
over fawq
  over there honaak
overtake yatakhaTa
oyster maHaar

package Tard
packet Aolbah
  a packet of … Aolbat …
  pack of cards shaddat waraq al-laAb
padlock qofl
page safHah
pain alam
paint (noun) dahaan
pair zawj
Pakistan baakestaan
Pakistani (man) baakestaanee
  (woman) baakestaaneeyah
  (adj) baakestaanee
pale momtaqeA
Palestine felasTeen
pancakes qoTaayef
paper waraq
paracetamol paraaseetamool
parcel Tard
pardon? Afwan?
parents waaledayn
park (noun) Hadeeqah
  where can I park?
  wayn awqef as-sayaarah?
party (celebration) Haflah
  (group) majmooAh
  (political) Hezb
passenger raakeb
passport jawaaz safar
pasta baasta
path mamsha
pavement raseef
pay yadfaA
peach khookh
peanuts fool soodaanee
pear komethra
118

pearl loo'loo'
peas besellah
pedestrian moshaah
peg (clothes) mashbak lel-ghaseel
pen qalam
pencil qalam rosaas
pencil sharpener mebrah lel-aqlaam
penfriend sadeeq moraaselah
peninsula shebh jazeerah
penknife meTwaah
people naas
pepper felfel
peppermints neAnaA
per: per night kol laylah
perfect kaamel
perfume AeTr
perhaps robbama
perm tamweej ash-shaAr
personal stereo 'walkman'
petrol banzeen
petrol station maHaTTat banzeen
petticoat tanoorah daakheleeyah
Pharaoh faraoon
photograph (noun) soorah
  (verb) yosawwer
photographer mosawwer
phrase book ketaab TaAbeeraat
piano biyaano
pickpocket nashaal
picnic nozhah lel-akl
piece qeTAh
pillow wesaadah
pilot (of aircraft) Tayaar
pin daboos
pine (tree) sanoobar
pineapple ananaas
pink wardee
pipe beebah
  (waterpipe: for smoking) ghalyoon
  (for water) anboob
piston makbas
pizza beetza
place makaan
plant nabaat

plaster *(for cut)* shareeт laaseq
plastic blaasteek
plastic bag shanтat blaasteek
plate тabaq
platform raseef
play *(theatre)* masraheeyah
please law samaнt
plug *(electrical)* qaabes
  (sink) sedaadah
pocket jayb
poison somm
police shorтah, boolees
police officer shorтee
police station noqтat ash-shorтah
politics siyaasah
poor faqeer
  (bad quality) radee'
pop music mooseeqee gharbee
pork laнm khanzeer
port *(harbour)* meenaa'
porter *(for luggage)* shayaal
  (hotel) bawaab
possible momken
post *(noun)* bareed
  (verb) yorsel
postbox sandooq bareed
postcard beтaaqah bareedeeyah
poster eAlaan
postman rajol bareed
post office maktab bareed
potato baтaaтes
poultry aт-тoyoor ad-daajenah
pound *(money)* jenayah
  (weight) raтl
powder boodrah
prawn jambaree
  (bigger) roobiyaan
prayer mat sejaadah sagheerah
  les-salah
prescription roosheттah
pretty *(beautiful)* zareef
  (quite) ela нadd ma
priest qasees
private khaas

problem moshkelah
  what's the problem?
  iyah al-moshkelah?
public Aam
pull yasнab
puncture thaqb
purple arjamaanee
purse kees
push yadfaA
pushchair Arabah leт-тefl
pyjamas beejaama
pyramids al-ahraamaat

Qatar qaтar
quality joodah
quay raseef al-meenaa'
question soo'aal
queue *(noun)* saff
  (verb) yaqef fee saff
quick sareeA
quiet haadee'
quite *(fairly)* ela нadd maa
  (fully) tamaaman

radiator raadiyaater
radio raadiyo
radish fejl
railway line kaтт as-sekah al-
  нadeedeeyah
rain maтar
raincoat meAтaf
raisins zabeeb
Ramadan ramaдaan
rare *(uncommon)* naader
  (steak) mashwee qaleelan
rat fa'r
razor blades shafrah
read yaqra'
reading lamp mesbaaн sagheer
ready mostaAedd
rear lights aдwaa' khalfeeyah
receipt 'eesaal

119

receptionist (*female*) mow<u>a</u>zzafat esteqb<u>aa</u>l
   (*male*) mow<u>a</u>zzaf esteqb<u>aa</u>l
record (*music*) 'os<u>ro</u>w<u>aa</u>nah
   (*sporting etc*) raqm qiy<u>aa</u>see
record player jeh<u>aa</u>z tashgh<u>ee</u>l al-'os<u>ro</u>w<u>aa</u>n<u>aa</u>t
record shop duk<u>aa</u>n bay_A al-'os<u>ro</u>w<u>aa</u>n<u>aa</u>t
red <u>a</u>Hmar
Red Sea al-b<u>a</u>Hr al-<u>a</u>Hmar
refreshments mor<u>a</u>rrab<u>aa</u>t
registered letter khe<u>ra</u>ab mos<u>a</u>jjal
relative qar<u>ee</u>b
relax yast<u>a</u>reH
religion deey<u>aa</u>nah
remember yataz<u>a</u>kker
   I don't remember laa ataz<u>a</u>kker
rent (*verb*) yast<u>a</u>'jer
reservation Hajz
rest (*remainder*) al-b<u>aa</u>qee
   (*relax*) ester<u>aa</u>Hah
restaurant m<u>a</u>rAM
restaurant car _Arabat al-m<u>a</u>rAM
return (*come back*) ya_A<u>oo</u>d
   (*give back*) yor<u>a</u>jje_A
return ticket tazk<u>a</u>rat zeh<u>aa</u>b wa-_A<u>oo</u>dah
rice ar<u>o</u>z
rich ghan<u>ee</u>
right (*correct*) saH<u>ee</u>H
   (*direction*) yam<u>ee</u>n
ring (*to call*) yat<u>a</u>sel bet-teleef<u>oo</u>n
   (*wedding etc*) kh<u>aa</u>tem
ripe n<u>aa</u>pej
river nahr
road sh<u>aa</u>re_A
rock (*stone*) s<u>a</u>khar
   (*music*) moos<u>ee</u>qa ar-r<u>oo</u>k
roll (*bread*) khobz
roof s<u>a</u>qaf
room gh<u>o</u>rfah
   (*space*) mak<u>aa</u>n
rope Habl

120

rose w<u>a</u>rdah
round (*circular*) d<u>aa</u>'eree
   it's my round en<u>a</u>ho d<u>a</u>wree
rowing boat m<u>a</u>rkab taqz<u>ee</u>f
rubber (*eraser*) memH<u>aa</u>h
   (*material*) kaootsh<u>oo</u>k
rubbish zeb<u>aa</u>lah
ruby (*stone*) yaaq<u>oo</u>t <u>a</u>Hmar
rucksack jaraband<u>ee</u>yah
rug (*mat*) sej<u>aa</u>dah sagh<u>ee</u>rah
   (*blanket*) b<u>a</u>ra<u>aa</u>n<u>ee</u>yah
ruins anq<u>aa</u>ᴅ
ruler (*for drawing*) m<u>a</u>s<u>ra</u>rah
rum room
run (*person*) y<u>a</u>jree
runway m<u>a</u>draj

sad Haz<u>ee</u>n
safe mam<u>oo</u>n
safety pin dab<u>oo</u>s am<u>aa</u>n
sailing boat m<u>a</u>rkab shor<u>a</u>_Aee
salad sal<u>aa</u>rah
salami sal<u>aa</u>mee
sale (*at reduced prices*) okazy<u>oo</u>n
salmon salam<u>oo</u>n
salt malH
same: the same dress nafs al-fost<u>aa</u>n
   the same people nafs al-ashkh<u>aa</u>s
   same again please nafs ash-shay' law sam<u>a</u>Ht
sand raml
sandals s<u>a</u>ndal
sand dunes kothb<u>aa</u>n raml<u>ee</u>yah
sandwich sandw<u>ee</u>tsh
sanitary towels Hef<u>aa</u>z al-H<u>a</u>yᴅ
sauce s<u>a</u>lsah
saucepan we<u>a</u>_A
Saudi Arabia as-sa_A<u>oo</u>d<u>ee</u>yah
sauna s<u>oo</u>na
sausage s<u>o</u>joq
say yaq<u>oo</u>l
   what did you say? shoo q<u>o</u>lta?
   how do you say...? kayf taq<u>oo</u>l ...?

scarf talfₑAh
  (*head*) mandeel ar-ra's
school madrasah
scissors maqass
scorpion Aqrab
Scotland eskotlanda
Scottish eskotlandee
screw masmaar molawwlab
screwdriver mafakk
sea baHr
seafood al-ma'koolaat
  al-baHreeyah
seat maqAd
seat belt Hezaam al-maqAd
second (*of time*) thaaniyah
  (*in series*) ath-thaanee
see yara
  I **can't see** laa 'ara
  I **see** (*understand*) fahₑmto
sell yabeeA
sellotape® seelooteep
separate (*noun*) monfasal
  (*verb*) yofassel
separated (*man*) monfasal
  (*woman*) monfasalah
serious khaTeer
serviette fooTah lel-maa'edah
several kameeyah
sew yokhayyet
shampoo shaamboo
shave (*noun*) Helaaqah
  (*verb*) yaHleq
shaving foam raghwat Helaaqah
shawl shaal
she heya
sheet sharshaf
shell sadafah
sherry sheree
ship safeenah
shirt qamees
shoelaces rebaaT al-Hezaa'
shoe polish warneesh aHzeeyah
shoes aHzeeyaH
shop dokaan

shopping tasawwoq
  to go **shopping** yatasawwaq
short qaseer
shorts banTaloon shoort
shoulder katef
shower (*bath*) dosh
  (*rain*) maTar
shower gel saboon jel
shrimp jambaree
shutter (*camera*) Haajeb al-Adasah
  (*window*) sheesh an-naafezah
sick (*ill*) mareeD
  I feel **sick** ashAor ka'enanee moshak
  Alal-ghathayaan
side (*edge*) Haafah
sidelights aDWaa' jaanebeeyah
sights: the sights of ... manaazer ...
silk Hareer
silver (*colour*) feDDee
  (*metal*) feDDah
simple baseeT
sing yoghannee
single (*one*) waaHed
  (*unmarried*) Aazeb
single room ghorfah be-sareer waaHed
sister okht
skid (*verb*) yanzaleq
skin cleanser monazzef lel-basharah
skirt tanoorah
sky samaa'
sleep (*noun*) nawm
  (*verb*) yanaam
  to go to **sleep** yanaam
sleeping pill Hoboob monawwemah
slippers shebsheb
slow baTee'
small sagheer
smell (*noun*) raa'eHah
  (*verb: transitive*) yashamm
smile (*noun*) ebtesaamah
  (*verb*) yodakhen
smoke (*noun*) dokhaan
  (*verb*) yabtasem
snack wajbah khafeefah

snorkel ash-shnorkel

snow thalj

so: so good jayyed jeddan
   not so much ela Hadd maa

soaking solution (for contact lenses)
   maHlool le-taTheer al-Adasaat al-laaseqah

socks jawaareb

soda water sooda

soft lenses Adasaat marennah

Somalia as-somaal

somebody shakhs maa

somehow be-Tareeqah maa

something shay' maa

sometimes aHyaanan

somewhere fee makaan maa
   son ebn

song 'oghniyah

sorry! aasef!
   I'm sorry ana aasef

soup shoorbah

south janoob

South Africa janoob efreekiya

South African (man) janoob efreekee
   (woman) janoob efreekeeyah
   (adj) janoob efreekee

souvenir tezkaar

spade (shovel) jaaroof
   (cards) al-bastoonee

spanner meftaaH sawaameel

spares qeTA ghiyaar

spark(ing) plug belajaat

speak yatakallam
   do you speak ...? hal tatakallam ...?
   I don't speak ... laa atakallam ...

speed sorAh

speed limit Hadd as-sorAh

speedometer Adaad as-sorAh

Sphinx aboo al-hool

spider Ankaboot

spinach sabaanekh

spoon malqaaH

sprain malakh

spring (mechanical) soostah
   (season) ar-rabeeA

122

stadium 'estaad

staircase solaalem al-mabna

stairs solaalem

stamp TaabeA

stapler dabaasah

star najmah
   (film) baTal al-felm

start (verb: intransitive) yabtade'

station maHaTTah

statue temthaal

steak befteek

steal yasreq
   it's been stolen laqad soreqat

steering wheel Ajalat al-qiyaadah

stewardess moDeefah

sting (noun) ladagh
   (verb) yaldogh
   it stings (hurts) towajjeA

stockings jawaareeb Hareemee

stomach maAedah

stomach ache alam al-maAedah

stop (verb) (transitive) yaqef
   (intransitive) yatawaqqaf
   (bus stop) maHaTTat baas
   stop! qeff!

storm AaSefah

strawberry faraawlah

stream jadwal

street shaareA

string (cord) doobaarah
   (guitar etc) watar

student Taaleb

stupid ghabee

suburbs DawaaHee

Sudan as-soodaan

sugar sokkar

suit (noun) badlah
   (verb) yonaaseb
   it suits you well enaha yonaasebak
   tamaaman

suitcase shanTat safar

sun ash-shams

sunbathing Hamaam shamsee

sunburn Haraqat shams

sunglasses nazaar<u>aa</u>t shams
sunny: it's sunny m<u>o</u>shreq ash-sh<u>a</u>ms
sunstroke Dar<u>a</u>bat ash-sh<u>a</u>ms
suntan l<u>a</u>fHat ash-sh<u>a</u>ms
suntan lotion maHl<u>oo</u>l Dedd ash-sh<u>a</u>ms
supermarket s<u>oo</u>perm<u>aa</u>rket
supplement joz' 'eD<u>aa</u>fee
sure mota'<u>a</u>kked
  are you sure? hal <u>a</u>nta mota'<u>a</u>kked?
surname al-l<u>a</u>qb
sweat (noun) <u>A</u>raq
  (verb) ya<u>A</u>req
sweet (not sour) H<u>o</u>lw
  (candy) H<u>a</u>lwa
swimming costume mal<u>aa</u>bes
  as-seb<u>aa</u>Hah
swimming pool Ham<u>aa</u>m seb<u>aa</u>Hah
swimming trunks maay<u>oo</u>
switch (light etc) meft<u>aa</u>H
Switzerland sw<u>ee</u>sra
synagogue m<u>a</u>Abad al-yah<u>oo</u>d
Syria soor<u>ee</u>yah

table T<u>aa</u>walah
tablet qors
take ya'khoz
takeoff 'eql<u>a</u>A
take off (plane) yoql<u>e</u>A
talcum powder b<u>oo</u>drat talk
talk (noun) Had<u>ee</u>th
  (verb) yataH<u>a</u>ddath
tall Taw<u>ee</u>l
tampon tamp<u>oo</u>n
tangerine y<u>o</u>sofee
tap sanb<u>oo</u>r
tapestry l<u>a</u>wHah kab<u>ee</u>rah taTreez<u>ee</u>yah
tea shaay
tea towel mensh<u>a</u>fah le-tajf<u>ee</u>f
  al-aw<u>aa</u>nee
telegram barq<u>ee</u>yah
telephone (noun) teleef<u>oo</u>n
  (verb) yat<u>a</u>ssel teleefoon<u>ee</u>yan
telephone box koshk teleef<u>oo</u>n

telephone call mok<u>aa</u>lamah
  teleefoon<u>ee</u>yah
television televeziy<u>oo</u>n
temperature Har<u>aa</u>rah
tent kh<u>a</u>ymah
tent peg w<u>a</u>ttad al-kh<u>a</u>ymah
tent pole A<u>mm</u>ood n<u>a</u>sb
  al-kh<u>a</u>ymah
than men
thank (verb) y<u>a</u>shkor
  thanks sh<u>o</u>kran
  thank you very much sh<u>o</u>kran jaz<u>ee</u>lan
that: that bus haz<u>aa</u>k al-b<u>aa</u>s
  that man haz<u>aa</u>k ar-r<u>a</u>jol
  that woman haad<u>ee</u>k al-H<u>o</u>rmah
  what's that? shoo haz<u>aa</u>k?
  I think that ... A<u>a</u>taqed an ...
their ...-hom
  their room ghorfat-hom
  their books kot<u>o</u>bhom
  it's theirs h<u>a</u>za m<u>e</u>lkhom
them: it's for them h<u>a</u>za l<u>a</u>hom
  give it to them A<u>a</u>Te<u>e</u>hom iy<u>aa</u>ha
then waqtz<u>aa</u>lek
there hon<u>aa</u>k
  there is/are ... fee ...
  is/are there ...? hal fee ...?
thermos flask t<u>o</u>rmos
these: these things haaz<u>e</u>he al-ashy<u>aa</u>'
  these are mine
  haaz<u>e</u>he al-ashy<u>aa</u>' m<u>e</u>lkee
they hom
thick sam<u>ee</u>k
thin raf<u>ee</u>A
think: I think so A<u>a</u>taqed
  I'll think about it s<u>a</u>wfa 'of<u>a</u>kker
  feel-mawD<u>OO</u>A
third ath-th<u>aa</u>leth
thirsty: I'm thirsty <u>a</u>na ATsh<u>aa</u>n
this: this bus h<u>a</u>za al-b<u>aa</u>s
  this man h<u>a</u>za ar-r<u>a</u>jol
  this woman h<u>a</u>zeh al-H<u>o</u>rmah
  what's this? m<u>a</u> h<u>a</u>za?
  this is Mr. ... h<u>a</u>za as-s<u>a</u>yed ...

those: those things
haazehe al-ashyaa'
  those are his
haazehe al-ashyaa'melk-ho
throat zawr
throat pastilles baasteeliya lez-zawr
through khelaal
thunderstorm Aasefah raAdeeyah
ticket tazkarah
tie (noun) rebaaT al-Aonoq
  (verb) yarboT
tights jawrab Hareemee
time waqt
  what's the time? kam as-saAh?
timetable jadwal
tin Aolbah
tin opener fataaHat Aolob
tip (money) baqsheesh
  (end) Taraf
tired taAbaan
  I feel tired ashAor be-taAeb
tissues mandeel waraq
to: to England ela engeltra
  to the station ela al-maHaTTah
  to the doctor ela aT-Tabeeb
toast khobz moHammaS
tobacco dokhaan
today al-yawm
together maAn
toilet towaaleet
toilet paper waraq towaaleet
tomato TamaaTem
tomato juice ASeer TamaaTem
tomorrow ghadan
tongue lesaan
tonic (for gin etc) tooneek
tonight haza al-masaa'
too (also) aydan
  (excessive) jeddan
tooth senn
toothache wajaA asnaan
toothbrush forshat asnaan
toothpaste maaJoon asnaan
torch mesbaaH yadawee

tour jawlah
tourist saa'eH
tourist office maktab as-siyaaHah
towel fooTah
tower borj
town madeenah
town hall daar al-baladeeyah
toy loAbah
toy shop dokaan loAb
track suit badlah let-tamreenaat
  ar-riyaaDeeyah
tractor jaraar
tradition taqaaleed
traffic moroor
traffic jam azmat moroor
traffic lights 'eshaaraat al-moroor
trailer Arabah maqToorah
train qeTaar
translate yotarjem
travel agency weqaalat safareeyaat
traveller's cheque sheek siyaaHee
tray seeneeyah
tree shajarah
trousers banTaloon
try yoHaawel
Tunisia toones
tunnel nafaq
Turkey torkeya
tweezers melqaaT
typewriter aalah kaatebah
tyre 'eTaar

umbrella shamseeyah
uncle (paternal) Amm
  (maternal) khaal
under taHt
underground taHt al-arD
underpants kalsoon
understand yafham
  I don't understand laa afham
underwear malaabes daakheleeyah
university jaameAh
unmarried ghayr motazawwaj

until Hatta
unusual ghayr Aadee
up fawq
  (upwards) be-'etejaah al-aAla
urgent Aajel
us: it's for us enaho lana
  give it to us aaTeena iyaaha
use *(noun)* faa'edah
  (verb) yastaAmel
  it's useless ghayr mofeed
useful mofeed
usual Aadee
usually Aadatan

vacancy *(room)* khaaleeyah
vacuum cleaner maknasah
  kahrabaa'eeyah
vacuum flask Tormos
valley waadee
valve semaam
vanilla al-faaneela
vase vaazah
veal betello
vegetable khoDarawaat
vehicle sayaarah
very jeddan
vest qamees taHtaanee
video tape shereet vidyoo
view manzar
viewfinder moHadded al-manzar
villa feelaa
village qoryah
vinegar khall
violin kamaan
visa veeza
visit *(noun)* ziyaarah
  (verb) yazoor
visitor zaa'er
  (tourist) saa'eH
vitamin tablet
  Hoboob veetaameen
vodka voodka
voice sawt

wait yantazer
waiter jarsoon
  waiter! ya jarsoon!
waiting room ghorfat al-entezaar
waitress jarsoonah
Wales waylz
walk *(noun: stroll)* tamashsha
  (verb) yamshee
  to go for a walk yatamashsha
wall Haa'eT
wallet maHfazah
war Harb
wardrobe doolaab
warm daafe'
was: I was ana konto
  he was howa kaan
  she was heya kaan
  it was kaanat
washing powder masHooq ghaseel
washing-up liquid saa'el ghaseel
  as-soHoon
wasp zanboor
watch *(noun)* saAh
  (verb) yoraaqeb
water miyaah
waterfall shalaal
wave *(noun)* mawjah
  (verb) yolaqqeA
we naHna
weather al-jaww
Web site mawqa Alal intarnet
wedding zefaaf
week 'osbooA
welcome marHaban
  you're welcome
  (don't mention it) al-Afw
Welsh men waylz
were: we were konna
  you were *(sing)* konta
  (pl) kontom
  they were kaanoo
west gharb
wet raTeb
what? maza?

wheel <u>a</u>jalah
wheelchair k<u>o</u>rsee be-ajal<u>aa</u>t
  lel-moq<u>ad</u><u>ee</u>n
when? m<u>a</u>ta?
where? ayn?
whether <u>e</u>mma
which? ay?
whisky w<u>ee</u>skee
white <u>a</u>by<u>a</u>d
who? man?
why? lem<u>aa</u>za?
wide ar<u>ee</u>d
wife z<u>a</u>wjah
wind r<u>ee</u>H
window shobb<u>aa</u>k
windscreen l<u>a</u>wHat az-zoj<u>aa</u>j
  al-amaam<u>ee</u>yah
wine nab<u>ee</u>z
wine list qaa'<u>e</u>mat an-nab<u>ee</u>z
wing jen<u>aa</u>H
with m<u>a</u>A
without bed<u>oo</u>n
woman H<u>o</u>rmah
women's toilet towaal<u>ee</u>t les-sayed<u>aa</u>t
wood khashab
wool s<u>oo</u>f
word k<u>a</u>lemah
work (noun) shoghl
  (verb) yasht<u>a</u>ghel
worry beads s<u>o</u>bHah
worse <u>a</u>rda'
worst al-<u>a</u>swa'
wrapping paper w<u>a</u>raq let-taghl<u>ee</u>f
wrist m<u>e</u>Asam

writing paper w<u>a</u>raq lel-ket<u>aa</u>bah
wrong kh<u>a</u>Ta'

year s<u>a</u>nah
yellow <u>a</u>sfar
Yemen: South Yemen al-y<u>a</u>man
  al-jan<u>oo</u>bee
  North Yemen al-y<u>a</u>man ash-shem<u>aa</u>lee
yes n<u>a</u>Am
yesterday ams
yet Hatt al<u>aa</u>n
  not yet l<u>a</u>ysa b<u>a</u>Ad
yoghurt zab<u>aa</u>dee
you (sing) <u>a</u>nta
  (pl) <u>a</u>ntom
  this is for you haz<u>e</u>he lak
  it's for you h<u>a</u>za lak
  with you m<u>a</u>Ak (m), m<u>a</u>Aek (f)
  your (sing) ...-ak
  (pl) ...-kom
  your book (sing) ket<u>aa</u>bak
  (pl) ket<u>aa</u>bakom
  your shoes (sing) Hez<u>aa</u>'ek
  (pl) Hez<u>aa</u>'ekom
yours: is this yours?
  (sing) hal h<u>a</u>za m<u>e</u>lkak?
  (pl) hal h<u>a</u>za melk-kom?
youth hostel bayt ash-sheb<u>aa</u>b
Yugoslavia yooghoslaav<u>ee</u>ya

zip s<u>oo</u>stah
zoo Had<u>ee</u>qat al-Hayaw<u>aa</u>n